Our Own Druidry

Also By
ADF Publishing

A World Full of Gods–John Michael Greer
Ogham, The Druid's Alphabet–Archdruid Robert (Skip) Ellison
Sacred Fire, Holy Well–Ian Corrigan
Deep Ancestors–Ceisiwr Serith

an introduction to Ár nDraíocht Féin
and the Druid Path

Our Own Druidry

ADF Publishing
P.O. Box 17874
Tucson, AZ 85731-7874

Assembled work copyright © 2009 Ár nDraíocht Féin
Respective articles copyrighted by their authors, used with permission

All rights reserved. No part of this book may be reproduced in any form or by any means without prior written consent of the publisher, excepting brief quotes used for review purposes.

First Printing May 2009

Printed in the United States of America

v1.5.09122009

Table of Contents

Book 1 : The Druid's Path — 9

Introduction — 11
- **The ADF Dedicant Path** — 12
  - Three Lights for Every Wisdom–Truth, Nature, Knowledge — 12
- **Three Triads of Practice** — 12
  - The First Triad of Druidic Teaching — 13
  - The Second Triad of Druidic Teaching — 14
  - The Third Triad of Druidic Teaching Ritual — 15
- **Concerning the Reading of Books** — 17
- **Additional Notes** — 18

Part 1. The Druid's Cosmos — 19
- ADF Cosmology and Sacrifice — 19
- Cultural Variations — 22
- Summary — 23
- New Druidic Triads — 23
- Nine Holy Things — 24
- The Two Powers — 26

Part 2. Basic Druidic Ritual — 29
- Your First Druidic Working — 29
- Tools of Druidic Ritual — 30
- A Simple Devotional — 31
- Brigantia's Celtic Devotions — 32
- A Simple Charm of Hallowing — 34

Part 3. Training the Mind — 35
- A Fire & Water Focusing — 35
- Simple Pre-Ritual Attunement — 36
- The Two Powers — 36
- Three Forms of Meditation — 37

Part 4. Attunement to Nature & The Kindred — 39
- The Basics — 40
- Opening Your Spirit to the Land — 40
- The Spirits in the Land — 41

Part 5. Simple Omens for Ritual — 45
- Sortilege — 45
- A Simple Method of Taking an Omen by Lot — 47

Part 6. The Very Basics of Ritual — 49
- Basics of Ritual — 50
- Working Ritual — 53
- A Solitary Self-Blessing Rite — 55
- Hearth Cultures & High Days — 60
- Summary — 72
- Working Ritual — 73

Part 7. A Working Full Druidic Ritual — 75
- The Outline of ADF Druidic Ritual — 75
- The Core Order of ADF Ritual for High Days — 77
- Items that ADF Rituals Do Not Include — 78

Book 2 : Deepening the Work — 79

Part 8. Lore & Essays — 81
- Right Action–A Pagan Perspective — 81
- Living the Good Life - Pagan Virtue — 84
- Nine Virtues of the Folk — 85
- The Nine Noble Virtues of Asatru — 86

Part 9. Personal Work — 87
- The Home Shrine — 87
- The Devotional Shrine — 88
- Three Bowls and a Stick: Creating a Home Shrine on a Budget — 88
- Druidic Mental Training — 93
- The Inner Work of the Simple Devotional — 96
- Passing the Mist — 98

Part 10. Walking the Path — 101
- The Intentions of Druidic Ritual — 101
- Practical Considerations — 103
- A Simple Rite of Offering at the Home Shrine — 104

Part 11. The High Days in Depth — 111
- Introduction to the High Days — 111
- Understanding the Practice of the High Days — 113
- Working the High Days — 114
- Conclusion — 116

Part 12. Personalizing Your Paganism — 117
- The Nature of The Gods & Spirits — 117
- Seeking the Hearth Gods — 118
- Choices and Expectations — 120
- Kindred Attunement Work — 120
- A Trance to Discover Hearth Gods — 121

Part 13. The Dedicant's Oath — 123
- A Dedicant's Oath Rite — 124

Appendices — 129

Appendix A: Recommended Reading Lists — iii
- **A Basic Reading List for Beginners** — iii
- **The Dedicant's Reading List** — iv
- **Additional Notes** — ix

Appendix B: Dedicant Path Documentation — xi

Appendix C: Adapting the Dedicant's Path to Specific Ethnic Paths — xv

Appendix D: Using the DP for Grove Building — xvii

Appendix E: Rune and Ogham Charts — xxviii
- **Rune Chart** — xxviii
- **Ogham Chart** — xxix

Book 1

The Druid's Path

Introduction

*Stand on a windswept hillside among the ruins of an ancient fortress
chanting songs seemingly pulled from the dragons beneath.*

*Raise your arms to the sky in a salute to the sun
perfectly framed by monolithic stones.*

Pound a drum to drive dancers onward as they ring a roaring bonfire.

*Slowly open your eyes and return to the two bowls
and a stick before you at your bedroom altar.*

Welcome to the path of the modern Druid! To walk it is to weave the ancient calling within you into the living world around you. This path asks you to study, to practice, and to grow closer to the many realms of power within and around you.

The work we introduce in the Dedicants Path will inspire and guide you as you build a personal Druidic practice. It will challenge and irritate you—we promise! You will have breakthroughs! You will also have moments of confusion and inertia. You will also find that we don't have all the answers you seek. However, if you manage to press on with actual practice and trust the simple methods offered here, the rewards come surely, if sometimes slowly.

It's been immortalized on posters, mouse pads and mugs: "A journey of a thousand miles begins with a single step." In this guide we strive to inspire you to that first step. We ask that you set aside the idea that you must properly 'prepare' to start on the Druid's path. We want you to know that the Gods, the Dead and the Spirits of Nature await you this very moment.

So go to the kitchen, and fill a bowl with water. Set up another bowl for a candle or incense. Set them in front of your favorite houseplant (or wooden spoon upended in a can of dirt) and enact the first ritual offered in this guide. Engage now with the 'other' whether you see it, feel it, hear it—or don't. And, in the doing, may your life be enriched and empowered over the days, weeks, years to come living YOUR in the doing, may your life be enriched and empowered over the days, weeks, years to come living YOUR Own Druidism.

The ADF Dedicant Path

Three Lights for Every Wisdom - Truth, Nature, Knowledge

Our Druidry is an effort to create Pagan ways that resemble those of the ancients, and serve the needs of modern students. A primary duty of any religious organization is to provide for the training and spiritual growth of its members, and any religious system is only as good as the training, skill and devotion of its members. ADF has developed a powerful and effective system of training Druidic students–the Dedicant's Path is the first step in this process. As ADF has grown, we have begun to evolve a consensus concerning symbolism, cosmology and practice. This small book presents an introduction to that consensus, and a basic guide to practicing Our Druidry.

The pattern of training presented here is based on widely-practiced methods of spiritual training, framed inside our understanding of ancient Pagan ways. These methods are simple, proven and reliable when practiced consistently. The outline of our training is considered core to our Druidic spirituality, but the specific articles in this edition should not be taken as exclusive doctrine. You are encouraged to adapt the work given here to your needs, within the basic outlines of our systems.

The Work is offered to our new members as a way to develop a meaningful and effective personal Paganism. It should be worked at whatever pace is comfortable to the student. An experienced Pagan, coming into our work from another system, could complete it in a year. A determined new student should expect to take a year or two. This cannot be 'workshop religion'–Druidry requires devoted personal practice and study to grow in our work.

The Path as taught in this guide is the basic training for practicing a Druidic Paganism that will bring you into closer communion with the Gods and Spirits, the Land, and with your own Spirit. The methods and rituals we give in this primer are enough to keep a steady practice through a whole life, even if you never choose further training in our work.

With this work in hand, the student has the tools to begin working a path of Druidic spiritual practice. The depth, and pace, of that work is up to each member's will and choice. From the first commitments to full, formal, personal practice, the Way is as open as the student is willing.

Three Triads of Practice

Druidry is a religion of the mind, of the heart, and of the flesh. Through our mind we learn the Old Lore, and we master vision and art. Through the heart we understand our fellow beings, and connect with the worlds. Through the flesh we experience the joy of life, and do our will in the manifest world. Our Dedicant Druid training is meant to engage each of these. Through study, meditation and trance we train the mind. Through virtue, meditation and attunement to the land, we open the heart. By knowing the land and celebrating ritual, we involve our bodies in our spiritual path. When the whole self is involved and trained, every kind of spiritual work is greatly enhanced.

The Dedicant's Work is divided into three triads of practice. These can sometimes be viewed as separate stages of the process, three grades or levels meant to allow students to approach the work of Paganism at their own pace. However, in practice, students work them at their own pace, eventually gaining all the skills if the work is done well.

The First Triad of Druidic Teaching

Virtue, Piety & Study

These three central principles and practices define all of Druidic spirituality. It is our hope that everyone who wishes to be considered a serious Druidic Pagan will devote themselves to them.

- **Virtue** is the duty of every person who wishes to live well within society. We consider the many things that the old lore has to teach about virtue, and do our best to apply our insights to our own lives.

- **Piety** is the duty we owe to the Gods and Spirits, for which They bless us in turn. When we choose to learn ritual, when we make our home shrines and altars, when we keep the customs and rites of the High Days, we bring piety to our work.

- **Study** is the duty we owe to ourselves—to grow by effort in strength, wisdom and love. To be more then we are when we begin, we must absorb new ideas, new methods and new goals—we seek these in both scholarship and the work of inspiration.

For many Pagans it may well be enough to pursue these goals in whatever ways are available, without much more formal practice. Right living, attendance at rites, honor to one's personal spirits, and pursuit of spiritual growth through study and practice can make for a full Pagan life.

Nine Pagan Virtues

- **Wisdom**: good judgment, the ability to perceive people and situations correctly, deliberate about and decide on the correct response.

- **Piety**: correct observance of ritual and social traditions; the maintenance of the agreements, both personal and societal, that we humans have with the Gods and Spirits. Keeping the Old Ways, through ceremony and duty.

- **Vision**: the ability to broaden one's perspective to have a greater understanding of our place/role in the cosmos, relating to the past, present and future.

- **Courage**: the ability to act appropriately in the face of adversity.

- **Integrity**: Honor; being true to one's self and to others, involving oath-keeping, honesty, fairness, respect and self-confidence.

- **Perseverance**: Drive; the motivation to pursue goals even when that pursuit becomes difficult.

- **Hospitality**: Acting as both gracious host and appreciative guest, involving benevolence, friendliness, humor, and the honoring of a gift for a gift.

- **Moderation**: Cultivating one's appetites so that one is neither a slave to them nor driven to ill health (mental or physical) through excess or deficiency.

- **Fertility**: Bounty of mind, body and spirit involving creativity and industry, an appreciation of the physical and sensual, nurturing these qualities in others.

The High Days

The most universal Druidic observance is the keeping of the Eight High Days. This calendar was devised early in the Neopagan movement as a synthesis of Celtic and other Indo-European holidays. As most widely-known among Pagans, the Eight High Days are:

- **The November Feast**: Samhain, the New Year, the Feast of the Dead
- **The Winter Feast**: Yule, the Longest Night
- **The February Feast**: Imbolc, Feast of the Goddess Brigid, first springtime
- **The Spring Feast**: Spring Equinox, Feast of Planting
- **The May Feast**: Beltaine, The Hinge of Summer, Feast of the Sidhe/Fairies
- **The Summer Feast**: Summer Solstice, The Feast of Labor
- **The August Feast**: Lughnasadh, Feast of the God Lugh, first harvest
- **The Fall Feast**: Fall Equinox, Feast of Reaping

In Our Druidry you will seek to keep each of these feasts in whatever way is good for you, from simple household customs to full Druidic rituals of worship.

The Second Triad of Druidic Teaching

The Hearth-Shrine, Mental Training, Attunement

The next group of teachings present the first steps in growing from common worship to trained practice of Druidic arts. They are primary skills which serve as the infrastructure for deeper and stronger personal practice.

- **The Home Shrine** is a dedication of actual space in one's life and home to the Work. Once you have learned the basics of our rites, the Shrine is the door to further ritual, your personal holy place.

- **Mental Training** is a dedication of one's own mind and will to the work. It is the door to vision, and the key to self-mastery. You will learn basic focusing for your early rites, with more to be learned as you go.

- The work of **Attunement** to nature is a dedication of one's time, affection and reverence. It teaches us about the Land on which we live, and is the door to effective relationship with the Gods and Spirits.

The techniques learned in this triad will serve the student for their entire life. This introduction can only offer the most basic introduction to these skills—skills central to any Pagan spiritual work. Few students will ever master these skills; it is the doing of the work itself that matters. The ever-present work of ritual, meditation and relationship builds Pagan spiritual life, for that life is not found in the wise words of others, nor in the high ideas of philosophers. It arises in the soul of everyone who really does the work. Wisdom, vision, understanding and compassion are the fruits of the tree of spiritual effort.

The Third Triad of Druidic Teaching Ritual

Full Personal Ritual, Hearth Paganism, The Dedicant's Oath

The final triad of the work takes the skills learned in the first two triads and applies them in specific ways. The skills begun in devotions and hearth rites and in the attunements are used in working full Druidic sacrifices. Working the full order of Ritual takes the student an important step toward personal priest/esshood. The ability to work full ritual adds depth and grace to personal religion, especially for solitary students and family hearths.

When the student has built skill at trance and meditation, has attuned her spirit to the land and the spirits, and can bring it all together in the sacred Nemeton, she can be said to have the skills of a Dedicated Druidic Pagan. The final phase of the program is a portal to the further work ahead. The techniques of seeking the Hearth Gods and Spirit Allies are a deepening and personalization of the techniques of land and spirit attunement.

The Rite of the Dedicant's Oath is a specialized application of those skills. It is a work of Pagan spiritual magic meant to both use and strengthen the skills that have been learned in seasonal and personal rites.

In some ways, choosing to develop the skills and practices of the Dedicant's Path through these steps is a definitive move away from the common world-view of modern times. One seeks real communion with spiritual beings outside the self, entering a mind-set in which non-physical beings can and will interact with mortals. As with each of the Dedicant Triads, the work of worship and relationship with the Gods, Goddesses and Spirits can be a lifetime's work. As in every step, the student should proceed at their own pace, letting the techniques merge with their personal practice naturally.

When the student feels confident in his Druidic skills, and feels that this path of virtue, study and practice is truly for him, he takes the Oath of Dedication. This Oath is, in fact, just the start of deeper spiritual work. In some ways it is the completion of the first round of formal Druidic training, but the work of the Dedicant Path remains the foundation and ongoing support of every kind of Druidic training that follows.

The commitments and practices that we have called the Dedicant's Path are not just a 'course', nor are they just 'training materials'. It is the whole work of core Pagan Druidic religion and spirituality, in broad, general steps. It offers every Druidic Pagan a level at which he or she can comfortably work, from the simple commitments of the First Triad, through the growth of the Second Triad to the personal clergyhood of the Third Triad. Beyond that work lies the greater world of spirit and magic, open to Dedicated Druids.

Becoming a Druidic Pagan–the First Oath, and the Hearth

ADF has an interesting history. Our work began in 1983 with large group rituals staged at public festivals by teams drawn from many parts of the country, and from a small group surrounding the first Archdruid in New York City. As a national organization we were a network tied together by newsletter and telephone. Local Groves came and went rather quickly in our first 5 or 6 years, often leaving the organization to continue a while on their own. At that time, ADF could hardly have been said to be a religion–we had few real core symbols, and little magical current. Our focus was outward, to the greater Pagan community, as we worked to attract our first wave of devoted leadership.

That first wave of leaders entered ADF from other Pagan paths. Several came out of traditional Wicca, or ceremonial magic, where they had spent years gaining magical skills. As this group applied their skills to the acorns of our ideas, the first solidly 'ADF-style' Groves began to grow, based directly on our

Order of Ritual and polytheological ideas.

After ten years, we had about a dozen strong Groves, and a growing synthesis of symbolism and ritual. We were developing the symbolic patterns and practices that turn a system from an exercise into a working religion. Members were beginning to find personal spiritual satisfaction in our work, and we developed the Dedicant's work as a first effort at teaching NeoPagan Druidry to individual members. Only now, it seems, are we reaching the stage where we can help solitary practitioners develop a Druidic spirituality of their own using our methods.

In retrospect, this might seem rather inverted. Starting from a national organization, we have slowly grown downward into effective local congregations. From that place we are prepared to grow downward again, to develop a network of solitary and small-group membership. It will be in the hearts and minds of individual practitioners, whether solitary or in Groves, that Druidic Paganism will finally reach its first full fruiting as a working religious system.

The Dedicant's work is the first effort at such training. Some years after the program was begun, though, it has become clear that it is only another step in our evolution. Some have found the DP to be ambitious, and it has become clear that we can help new students by giving them a simpler introduction to the practice of Our Druidry.

The First Oath

Our Druidry can appear rather daunting to those taking a first look at us. We propose new ritual paradigms, challenge Pagans to take up scholarly study, and suggest real devotion to real Gods. So it seems wise to focus the attention of new students on our most core values, offering some direction, while leaving personal work open-ended.

When a student has examined our way's work and worth sufficiently to satisfy herself, and is prepared to make a personal commitment to Druidic Paganism as at least a part of her spiritual path, then it is time for the First Oath. This oath is made not to ADF as an organization, nor is it given to our Archdruid, or to any local leader. The First Oath is between the student and her Gods and Spirits.

In the First Oath the student pledges to take up the Three Ways that are the core of our work:

1 **Virtue**: to do right and live well

2 **Piety**: to keep the customs and work of the Pagan Way

3 **Study**: to seek to increase Pagan knowledge and skill

At this stage there is no need to define any particular fulfillment of these virtues, though the Dedicant's material gives the basics. Interpretation can be left to the individual, or to whatever local consensus might develop. In time we will develop a body of writing that will help new members begin their spiritual quest for the blessings of Pagan Druidry.

Here is an example of what a First Oath might say:

*"I, [Name], before this assembly, declare myself to be a Pagan,
a seeker of the Old Ways, a worshipper of the Elder Gods.*

*With this holy oath I set my foot upon the path, the Druid's
Way, and I vow to make my dedication plain.*

*I vow to seek virtue in my life, to do right by my kin, my
friends and my community, I vow to make my Paganism
real, by keeping the rites and works that call to me.*

*I vow to deepen my understanding of the Ways through study
to fill my mind with the truth of the Elder Paths.*

*These things I swear to the Gods, with those
gathered here as my witnesses. So be it."*

With the First Oath completed, the student can feel themselves to be a part of a definite community, whether local or distant—the community of sworn Pagans.

We need not set standards for the fulfillment of this oath. It stands as a personal, individual commitment that need not be measured by an organization. It might, however, give leadership a basis on which to build the work of members. Local programs for new members, and support material for solitaries, might be organized into one of these three core modes.

For many Pagans this level of involvement may be sufficient. To seek virtue, to be as pious as our life allows, and to increase, however gradually, one's knowledge is as much religion as many will need.

We might hope, however, that many others will be drawn toward a deeper practice. The next triad of the Dedicant's work–the home shrine, meditation and nature contacts–opens naturally before them. Those who are prepared to make a shrine in their homes, who want to begin to grow a personal Paganism in their lives, can take the Oath of the Hearth.

The Hearth Oath

Many who choose to work as solitary Pagans seek the skills and, one might say, the authority to function as their own 'priest' or 'priestess'. We may agree that there is no intrinsic need for external validation of a person's spiritual work. That said, the goal of ADF has always been to provide a structure into which that personal work can be fit, and the training needed to use that structure effectively. We can usefully offer a formal step in which our students can choose to formally take up the work of building a personal Paganism.

The Hearth Oath is a statement by the Pagan that they will formally take up the worship of the Gods and Spirits proper to their hearth. This will fit nicely with the second Triad of the Dedicant's work. The student establishes his home shrine, slowly acquiring or making the Hallows needed for full personal rites. He learns to manage his mind, and begins seeking the spirits in the local land that may be his allies.

Ancient Paganism was decentralized. There were no weekly communal gatherings at places of group worship–no 'churches'. Instead, Paganism was based at the hearths of clans and families. Each garth, each steading, would have had its household God/desses, the deities of the professions followed by its folk, of the prosperity of land and herd, the inspiration of the clan's spirit. Those members who wish to move their own practice beyond the basic involvement of the First Oath are encouraged to declare their Hearth as hallowed to the Old Ways, and to begin building their personal Hearth Religion.

Concerning the Reading of Books

The ancient Druids made themselves repositories of knowledge, as well as seekers of wisdom. We hear of their twenty years of learning, taught by word of mouth, without written support for much of the work. In our time we cannot spend the afternoon beneath the oaks, listening to the teachers. Instead, we must read books. Books are the voices of wisdom, though we must choose them wisely. The work of study is a spiritual work in the path of wisdom, and we hope you will make the acquisition of knowledge about the Old Ways a sort of spiritual duty. It is good to develop the habit of reading diligently, one book followed by another. That habit will keep you learning and growing through your whole life. It should no more be neglected than your meditations.

We offer two book lists in **Appendix A**. The first consists of popular introductions and instructions –books likely to be found in Pagan bookstores and 'occult' sections of major booksellers. They are not scholastic studies, but will give basic and reliable material. The second is the official Dedicant Reading List.

It contains core mythic and lore material for several ethnic Paganisms, and good summaries of history and background. Those who choose to do the formal documentation for the Dedicant's Path must read three books from that list (for complete requirements to complete the Dedicant's Path, please see **Appendix B**).

Additional Notes

We recommend that the beginning student avoid any nonfiction by Robert Graves, D.J. Conway, Lewis Spense, H.P. Blavatsky, Edward Williams (aka Iolo Morganwg), or any works by others based on their writings, or those of Merlin Stone, Barbara Walker, or other revisionist ideologues. Some of the assertions made in these sources can't be supported by current scholarship on the Druids; the use of common sense and a critical eye are highly recommended in dealing with these books (and all books for that matter).

This is not to say that they don't have their own possible worth or that people shouldn't know about these books, but that an understanding of these writers should come after understanding Druidry/Neopaganism in general. One has to get a firm grounding, four walls and a roof before she can decide on what kinds of curtains to look at.

When in doubt, consult your nearest tree…

Part 1

The Druid's Cosmos

In religion, cosmology is, essentially, the study of the universe–how it is structured and how the various parts interact with each other to create a cohesive whole. In ADF, we have studied the ideas and beliefs of the ancient Indo-Europeans, and have found similarities which seem to occur across many of these cultures. These common ideas can be assembled into a coherent system that reflects the ideas of the ancients while providing us with the structure needed to create our Core Order of Ritual.

While we cannot claim that all IE cultures shared all these ideas, we have found that they do fit in well in most IE Pagan cultural contexts.

ADF Cosmology and Sacrifice

Chaos and Cosmos

To the ancient Proto-Indo-Europeans, the only part of their world that they could reasonably control was their own encampment, and perhaps the fields immediately around it where they kept their cattle. But out beyond those fields were unknown steppes or forested lands populated by wild animals, ghosts and hostile tribes. This outer, terrifying land they called chaos. Cosmos, on the other hand, means order, and the cosmos of these early tribes consisted of those things they could rely on–such as their encampments, their warriors' prowess, their cattle, the seasons and the great, annual dance of the stars across the sky as they circle the Pole Star.

Chaos is not always negative, for from outside the boundaries of Order come resources, and mysteries, and some of the inspiration and wisdom of the Gods.

In looking at the world around them, the ancients saw the tension between chaos and cosmos, and the opportunities and risks it offered. They created ritual to manage the relationship between the tribe and the 'Other' (those things outside the tribe), between the village and the wildwood, and between chaos and cosmos.

The Creation of the Universe

We do not know of one, single IE myth used by the ancients to explain the creation of the Universe. As the Indo-Europeans migrated across Asia and Europe, many of them were influenced by neighboring cultures, and these influences may have changed their original mythic beliefs. However, some diverse IE cultures share a similar creation myth that many scholars believe may reflect the original myth from Proto-Indo-European times.

In these ancient IE myths, first there were two beings, Man and his Twin (sometimes accompanied by a cow). Man sacrificed or slew Twin and used the parts of his body to create the universe as we know it. In some myths, Twin colonized the Underworld and became the first God of the Dead. Thus, the cosmos was established out of chaos, and the sacred was manifested there. This first sacrifice shows that, since the Worlds are all made of one being, there must be a basic kinship between all beings, and communication must be possible between the Worlds.

The Three Worlds

In general terms, the ancients saw the universe divided up into three Worlds that we use in ADF.

The Heavens (or Upperworld) is the place of order, where the Shining Ones dwell. The predictable dance of the stars around the Pole Star shows great order, and the bright, shining sky forever exists above the storms and clouds of the Midworld.

The Midworld is the world in which we live, the place of the Spirits of the Land and of life as we know it. And here also are the Otherworlds, the mythic/spiritual counterparts to our common world, existing unseen all around us. These are the homes of the greater land spirits, such as the Sidhe, the Tylwyth Teg, the Wights, and the Dryads, etc.

The Underworld is the shadowy land of the Dead and of the chthonic deities. Here, below the surface of the Midworld, the dead, or at least their bones, are buried, and this is where their spirits dwell. Death is a reminder that the wonderful order of life soon ends in the chaos of dissolution. But the Underworld is also a source of wonderful fertility, and especially of the inspiration that arises from the wisdom of the Dead. In some cultures, the Underworld is also seen as being islands across the western sea.

The Sacred Center of the Worlds

In ritual, we do as the Gods did by re-creating the creation of Cosmos and of the universe. In so doing, we also re-create the time and place of that first creation.

The Sacred Center is that place created in ritual where all the Worlds meet, and where a "portal" can be opened, allowing communication between these cosmic planes. In this place, we can be in all Worlds at once and in all times at once. Here, anything is possible.

In ADF worship, we do not seek to transport worshippers between the Worlds to celebrate our rites, rather we open a Gate between the Worlds.

The Triple Hallows

In order to re-create the sacred center of the Worlds, we need first to connect to those Worlds. In ritual, we bless the symbols of the Well, Fire & Tree (the Triple Hallows) in our ritual spaces to create gateways to these spiritual places. While the symbols of Well, Fire & Tree are the ones most commonly used in ADF (and Fire is required), there are some accepted cultural variations such as Pit/Fire/Portal, three Fires, etc.

Fire—The Fire is the ancient focus of ritual. It is the transmuter and transformer, which can take something, like oil or butter, and change it into something else, something possibly more accessible to the Gods. The Fire corresponds with the Shining Ones and Order, and serves as a connection to the world of the Heavens. The Fire is common to all IE cultures.

Well—The Well is an ancient place of offering. The ancient Celts used to offer weapons, precious objects and even household goods to water. The Well connects with the earth power beneath us, and with the fresh, ordered waters of the Earth. It corresponds with the Sacred Dead and with the chthonic deities, and is our connection to the Underworld. The Well can also be seen as a shaft, pit or chasm.

Tree—The Tree is the axis mundi or axis of the world. It is the cosmic pillar that holds up the sky and connects, through its roots, with the lands below our feet. Thus the Tree, while existing in the Midworld, connects all the Worlds above and below. It can be a tree, a mountain, an omphalos or even a pillar or boundary stone. But the Tree always stands at the center of 'our' world.

Liminal Gods and Psychopomps

In ADF ritual, once we have re-created the Center of the Worlds and consecrated the Hallows, we call upon a special, liminal God or Goddess to "join their magic with ours" so that we might open those gateways to the Three worlds that have taken form in our Hallows. We call these deities Gatekeepers.

Liminality is the condition of being neither one thing nor another. In the physical world, liminal objects can be boundaries of all kinds, such as walls, hedges, and sea shores or even a place like a crossroads, that is neither one road nor another, or both at once. Liminal times include dawn and dusk (neither day nor night) or even, for the Celts at least, the hinge days of Beltane and Samhain (neither summer nor winter). The veils between the Worlds are thinnest at liminal times and places.

Certain deities are particularly known for crossing the boundaries between the Worlds. Some carry folks into Faery, while others carry the dead to the Underworld or the Isles of the Blest. These latter deities are also called psychopomps.

*ghosti

This word, *ghosti, is a reconstructed Proto-Indo-European word that refers to "someone with whom one has reciprocal duties of hospitality." The English words 'guest' and 'host' both come from *ghosti. Another way of putting this would be the saying, "I give that You may give," and this concept underlies our entire religion. We give offerings to the Kindreds to form relationships with them, just as we would give of ourselves to our friends and family, to maintain close ties. In ancient days, folks would build friendship by the ritual exchange of gifts, and these ties could bind families for generations. And so we give to the Kindreds in expectation that They will give to us in return.

Sacrifice

In our time, the word 'sacrifice' has a negative connotation to some people, due to its use by the dominant religion to refer to its founder's agonizing death by execution.

But the word comes from the Latin words sacer (sacred; to set apart) and facere (to make or to do). Thus its true meaning is "to make sacred, to set apart." And this is just what we do when we make our offerings to the Kindreds. And when we make these offerings, we are 'setting them apart' from the profane world, making them appropriate for the Kindreds.

There are a number of reasons for making sacrifice:

* Reciprocity–I give so that You may give. This is one of the most common forms of sacrifice in ADF. We make offerings to the Kindreds in order to receive blessings or wisdom in return.

* Apotropaic Offerings–Averting evil or bad luck. Here, the sacrificer makes an offering to say, in effect, "Take this and go", rather than to form a relationship with that Power. The removal of any ritual pollution would also come under this heading.

* The Shared Meal–Here we take food and eat some while giving the rest to the Kindreds. This act enhances the unity of the People through celebration, and allows communion with the Kindreds.

* Maintaining the Cosmic Order–When we give offerings that the unity of the people be enhanced, or the earth may be healed and strengthened, we are re-affirming the cosmic order.

* Chaos Mitigates Cosmos–Too much order can cause brittleness.

Think of a tree that cannot bend in the wind, and therefore breaks. In our rites, we have Praise Offerings, which cannot be totally controlled. Spontaneity in prayers, actions and praise can keep a ritual from becoming lifeless.

Cultural Variations

There are many different ways that the various hearth cultures of ADF interpret the Three Worlds and the Triple Hallows. Here we will only cover three of them, but other information may be found on the pages or e-mail lists of the various Kins in ADF.

Celtic (Irish)

Uisnech was the cosmological center of Ireland. Here the Druid Mide built the first fire in Ireland that burned for seven years, and from which all hearth fires in the land were lit. There was also a pillar stone at Uisnech which had five sides, representing the five provinces of Ireland. The twelve chief rivers were also said to have come from Uisnech, either caused by a storm or flowing from the white-rimmed well there. Other Irish wells are said to be the sources of various rivers, and the one at the source of the river Boyne had hazel trees that dropped their nuts into the pool, where they were eaten by the salmon of knowledge.

Instead of the Three Worlds of Heaven, Midworld and Underworld, the Irish thought of the cosmos as the Three Realms of Sky, Land and Sea. The sea was equated with the Underworld because the Dead would journey to the distant islands of the West beyond the mists of the sea, where the sky and ocean touched. Most Irish Celtic Groves in ADF use the Well, Fire, and Tree for the Hallows.

Germanic/Norse

Instead of three Worlds, the Norse have nine. While Asgardhr and Vanaheim, Midgardhr, and Helheim may correspond well with Heaven, Midworld and Underworld, respectively, the other five worlds are more problematical.

Ljossalfheimr (Alfheimr), the land of the Light Alfs, might fit in well with the Heavens, while Svartalfheimr, land of the dwarves (whose names translate into things like "dead one" and "corpse"), and Niflheim, the world of ice, may be part of the Underworld (Helheim may even be within Niflheim).

Svartalfheimr may also be in the Midworld, as the caves and tunnels of the dwarves are directly below the earth. The other two worlds (Jotunheimer, land of Giants, and Muspellheim, realm of the Fire Giants) may also fit into the Midworld part of the ADF cosmos.

Yggdrasill, the great World Tree, is at the center of the Worlds and connects them all. Odin, from his seat, could see all the Worlds at once, suggesting that it may have been on Yggdrasill. At the World Tree's base are three Wells, Mimir's Well (connected with knowledge), Wyrd's Well (connected with the court of the Aesir) and Hvergelmir, where the serpent Nidhogg would chew at the root of Yggdrasill. Mimir's Well could be a connection to the Ancestors, as a source of knowledge and wisdom. And Fire, the great transmuter and transformer, takes sacrifices to the Spirits.

Hellenic

In Hellenic religion, a mountain (and possibly Mt. Olympos, home of the 12 main Gods), might best correspond with the Heavens. The world of men and of the land and tree spirits, such as centaurs and dryads, would be the Midworld, and Hades, the land of the Dead, fits in well with the Underworld.

The Triple Hallows of Well, Fire & Tree in Hellenic religion could be conceived of as Pit, Fire and Mountain. A Mountain (again, possibly Olympos itself) could be the connection with the Heavens (though an Omphalos might work as well) and a Pit or chasm could be the connection to the Underworld (also, libations to the dead were often poured into holes specially made in the roofs of tombs, for the dead were ever thirsty). The Fire, seen as the Goddess Hestia, is that central point here in the Midworld where everything comes together, and where transformation is possible.

Summary

Regardless of our various hearth cultures, the cosmology of ADF works to bring us together in ritual and as a religion. Our Core Order of Ritual is based on this cosmology and the ideas from which it springs. We all re-create the cosmos to establish the Sacred Center, allowing communication with the three Worlds or Realms. We make sacrifices to the Kindreds, ask for Their blessings in return, and wind down the rite, disestablishing the Sacred Center in the process. You can see the article on ritual elsewhere in this booklet for a more complete explanation of our Core Order.

New Druidic Triads

Three Triads of the Worlds

1. **Three Realms**
   Underworld - the Cauldron of Rebirth
   Midrealm - the Cauldron of Bounty
   Heavens - the Cauldron of Wisdom

2. **Three Worlds**
   The Sea - the Wild Waste - the Road to the Blessed Isles
   The Land - the Green Earth - Dwelling of Many Kins
   The Sky - the Unchanging Order - the Place of the Shining Ones

3. **Three Kindreds**
   The Dead - the Blessed Ancestors - who sustain the Clans
   The Nature Spirits - the Other Kins - who sustain the Web of the Worlds
   The Deities - Eldest, Wisest and Mightiest - who sustain All

ADF's cosmology was created for us–the people of today. We have not attempted to re-create ancient religions because we are not ancient peoples. Rather, we are modern people worshipping ancient Gods and Goddesses in modern times. Seen in this light, all of our hearth cultures can function well within ADF, bringing us all together as one Folk.

Three Triads of Ritual

1. **Three Gates**
   The Well - the Deep Gate - the Sustainer
   The Fire - the Bright Gate - the Transformer
   The Tree - the All-Boundary - the Connector

2. **Three Tools**
   The Cauldron - Source of Wisdom, Love and Power
   The Wand - the Poet's Skill, the Wizard's Will
   The Cloak/Ring/Robe/Lamen- the Mantle of Magic, encompassing Spirit.

3. **Three Deeds**
   The Grove - Arriving; Honoring the Three; Opening the Gates
   The Sacrifices - to the Kindreds; to the Patrons; to All
   The Blessing - Asking; Receiving; Thanking

Nine Holy Things

These nine concepts make up the core Druidic understanding of the order of the cosmos. They are wide, deep symbols, that will repay study and meditation. These simple statements are presented as a starting place on the journey to comprehend the great triskelion that encompasses all.

Three Realms

Within and behind all apparent reality is the Otherworld.

* **Underworld**: The power under the Earth is called the 'chaos of potential.' The underworld realms are the place of the ancestors, of the Daoine Sidhe, of the underworld gods and goddesses. From their halls and lands issue bounty and new life, the wisdom of memory, and the root of personal strength. The underworld is associated with water, both the sea and the waters under the Earth. This water is the rich nutrient soup into which all individual existence dissolves and from which it arises. So it is sometimes called, or symbolized by, the cauldron of rebirth.

* **Midrealm**: The midrealms are the setting of the great tales. In the middle lands dwell all the mortal kins, and a variety of spirits as well. The common world where human and nonhuman Kindreds live, the land, sea and sky, are reflected in the middle worlds, hung between underworlds and heavens. Some of the gods and goddesses dwell there, near to their mortal children, and sometimes mighty ancestors make a home in the middle lands to aid their descendants The midrealm is associated with the surface of the land, the home of the hosts, and with the many spirit tribes that share it with us. It is the spirit-matrix that underlies the common world in which we dwell, its twin and its mirror. Within it grows every individual manifestation of life, and so it is called the cauldron of bounty.

- **Heavens**: The power of the overworld is the pattern of the world order. The heavenly realms are the places of the brightest gods and goddesses, the Shining Ones, and those mortal heroes who have been welcomed into their palaces. From the revolving castle of the sun, moon and stars comes the pattern of existence, the wisdom of perspective and the objective eye, and clarity of thought and will. The heavens are associated with the sky, and with the sacred fire the that brings the heavens' light into the grove. This light is the catalyzing quickener that calls individual forms and beings out of the chaos of potential. When it shines in the soul it brings the pearls of idea from the sea of mind, and so it is called the cauldron of wisdom.

Three Worlds

The middle realm is divided in a pattern related to the three realms, another reflection of the holy triskel.

- **Land**: The land is the common earth upon which we dwell, our mortal home and support. It is the tilled field and the unseen mountain-top, swamp and desert, town and woodland. The land is the convergence of sea and sky, the holy island. It is connected to the otherworlds through caverns and deep places, wells, pools and the tops of high places. The land is the home of those animal kins that are closest to our human life, our allies and our predators.

- **Sea**: Surrounding our island home on every side is the boundless expanse of the oceans. The sea is the mystery, the portion of the human world most alien to humankind. Within its misty vastness may be found islands of wonder and fear, the isles of the otherworlds is the home of the cattle of Tethra, the uncounted fishes and their stranger cousins and kin. Some of those are friends to human folk, and some are not.

- **Sky**: Arching above our common land and sea is the blue dome of the sky, the realm of cloud and storm and calm breezes. It is the airy realm that is both all around us and far beyond our reach. In its floating worlds of clouds we see the playgrounds of the gods, the seats from which they watch the world. From the sky's high distances descend the birds, so often the messengers of the gods.

Three Kindreds

Within this cosmos of three and three dwell the Gods and the non-gods–the three Kindreds.

- **The Shining Ones**: In the first days the Mother of All bore children, the people of the Mother, who are our Gods and Goddesses. They are the first family, the eldest and wisest, their youth continually renewed by their magical feasts. They are the kings and queens, the magicians and the poets, the powers of love and delight, the warriors, and the cow women, the smiths and all the powers of the wild. In every culture, the gods and goddesses guide their mortal children. Each Pagan culture has a family of deities whose wisdom, love and power sustain the worlds and humankind. Whether these cultural forms portray separate, individual entities; or whether they are names and titles of one great family of gods and goddesses, they are the object of our highest worship, and are our greatest allies.

- **The Ancestors**: Many tales tell us that humankind is descended from, and intermarried with, the Gods and Goddesses. The fire of the heavens and the dark waters of the underworld flow in our human spirits, and death cannot extinguish us. So we remember and honor the ancestors, the Mighty Dead. The old lore makes it clear that human spirits sometimes reincarnate in the mortal world, often in their own family bloodline. But it is equally clear that many of the dead are 'reborn' in the otherworld, in the land of the dead. There they live the lives their fate has woven for them, just as we do here. Pagan tradition teaches that the ancestors hear the voice of the living, that they value our worship and offerings. It teaches that the mighty dead still have power in the mortal world, to guide and protect, or to chastise. So we make our gifts to them, and listen closely for their voices.

- **The Nature Spirits**: Humankind and our ancestors share the worlds with a myriad of other beings, other forms of life both physical and spiritual. The other kins share with us and the gods and goddesses in the weaving of the web of fate. They are as various as the species of our world, filled with magic and skill and cunning. Some of them are the beast-spirit peoples. Many of these are close allies of human folk, the hound and bull and pig and more. Others are of the deep wild, the wolf and deer and boar. The spirits of birds go freely between Earth and sky. Other spirits are the wonder peoples, the magic races of the many cultures–fauns and dryads, Alfar and Daoine Sidhe. They roam in midrealm countries sometimes very close to ours, sometimes very distant. We honor them and sometimes seek their aid in magic.

The Two Powers

The Underworld Power

The primary image that evokes the underworld power is of the waters that seep, pool and flow beneath the surface on which we dwell. These waters are in some way connected with all the world's waters, an ever-flowing current. In that water is dissolved every nutrient required to sustain all life, nutrients derived from the natural processes of decay and dissolution. From this matrix every being arises, all the bounty of the world. Even crystal condenses from the waters under the Earth.

In Celtic lore this primal water can be connected with the primal Mother–Danu, Mother of the gods and goddesses. She can be envisioned as the ocean of undifferentiated awareness, her mind the ever-flowing current of being deep beneath our surface life. Every individual manifestation is rooted and connected through the waters of the 'all-mind.'

When we contact the underworld power we reach deep into the dark, to the current from the past, to the flow and store of the memory of the worlds, the undifferentiated flow of possibility that is sometimes called the 'chaos of potential.' Through our underworld awareness we can reach out to touch the roots of other minds, other forms of consciousness. We grasp the raw material, that can be shaped by magic into new forms and manifestations.

The Heaven Power

The primary image that evokes the heaven power is the light of sun and moon, the great lights that wheel and turn in their eternal order. When this power falls upon the earth it draws forth individual lives, stirring and transforming the potentials of the waters, providing the pattern that allows individual existences to grow. In the same way, this heaven power is made real to us in fire. Just as the sun warms the waters of the earth, so the sacred fire warms the contents of the magic cauldron, transforming raw materials into food, medicine or sorcery.

In Celtic lore this primal fire can be connected with the first Father, Bel, the ancestor of the Gods and Goddesses. He can be understood as the spark of kindling, the point around which individual beings grow from the matrix of potential. He inspires the creative power that allows us to shape reality from the river of fate.

When we contact the heaven power we feel the inner light, the precipitating, crystallizing force that makes us who we are. We grasp the organizing pattern of cosmos, that allows continuity of form and life, which can be called the world order. Through heavenly awareness we gain the power of shaping, that orders the flow of potential, that allows us to bind fate to some small degree, according to our will.

These two powers are the dynamic tension that produces our apparent reality. They are present in every being, every spirit. In humankind they flow in our bodies and souls, and can be directed to some extent by will and imagination, or by emotion and its accompanying impulses. So the student learns to become aware of the two powers as they flow in the worlds and in herself. She learns to use will and vision to accumulate the powers in body and soul, and to draw strength from them. From this skill many kinds of practical magic arise, beginning with the power of the gate, the place at the boundary between heaven and the underworld.

Part 2

Basic Druidic Ritual

Your First Druidic Working

Here is a simple ritual that can be prepared and performed easily. It is meant to affirm your presence on the Path, and convey a simple blessing. It can be used at any time as a simple devotional moment.

You will need a flame, a bowl of water with a piece of silver, and a cup of drink.

Place the flame and the bowl next to one another, with the cup between them.

Drop the silver into the water, and say:

The bounty of the Deep

Light the flame, and say:

The rising of the Light

Place a drop of water on your forehead. Keeping your body relaxed, concentrate on the feel of the water on your skin. Let it fill your awareness.

Focus your gaze on the flame. Let the form and light of the fire be the concentration of your vision.

Take three deep breaths, holding the concentrations on the feeling of the water and the vision of the fire, then say:

Between Fire & Water, I find my balance.

Take up the cup, and raise it in salute to the Holy Powers of the world, saying:

I drink to the Holy Powers of the world
I drink to the Ancestors (sip the drink)
I drink to the Landspirits (sip the drink)
I drink to the Shining Goddesses and Gods (sip the drink)

> *To all the beings, in all the worlds*
> *In Land, Sea and Sky,*
> *Below and on high*
> *I drink this cup of fellowship. (drink the rest of the cup)*

Pause in silence for a time, allowing the feelings that the rite produces to be felt.

When you are ready, place a drop of water on your forehead. Focus your gaze on the flame, then say:

> *Between Fire & Water, I find my balance.*

Extinguish the flame, and say:

> *The Light rises in me.*

Take the silver from the water and say:

> *The Deep flows in me.*
> *This work is complete!*
> *The Heavens shine above me,*
> *The Deeps flow below me.*
> *I stand amidst all realms,*
> *And go forth with the blessing of the Kindreds.*

Tools of Druidic Ritual

Druid ritual, at its simplest, requires only a fire, a bowl of water, and any specific things called for by the work. Under an ancient tree, beneath the moon a skilled priest or priestess can do any magic. Yet, both we and the ancients love beautiful things properly arrayed, so we build temples and shrines, make vessels and tools of spiritual art. All of these things bring added blessings and power to our work.

Sacred fire must be present at any full sacrifice, and should be used even in simple devotions. In the most reduced circumstances a single candle may serve, with offerings of sticks or cones of incense. A censer can hold charcoal blocks to receive offerings of scented oil or herbs, perhaps with a ring of nine candles around it. This is best for indoor rites when no hearth is available. Of course, the best fire is lit outdoors, campfire style. To light a good fire, you will need three types of wood. Tinder is made from tiny slivers of wood, dry grass and herbs, or bark. Kindling is small, finger-sized pieces that catch from the tinder, and fuel is larger wood that holds the flame. You will need about five times as much kindling as fuel to see you through a sacrifice.

The well is the vessel used to hold the magic waters in ritual. It is a reflection of the triple cauldron of bounty, healing and wisdom, which in turn reflects the primal well of wisdom. Traditional cauldrons are round, three-legged cooking pots of iron or brass. They can also be found made of ceramic material. The cauldron must always be clean enough that you could drink from it.

Holy water can be made of water from three natural sources–local lakes, running streams, blessed wells if they can be found. These combined waters should be exposed to the light of sun, moon and sacred fire or lightning. Holy water could be stored in a tightly closed vessel and added in small amounts to the larger amounts of regular water used for ritual.

The offering bowl is a vessel that receives offerings to the earth during indoor rituals.

The horn or chalice is a drinking vessel used for pouring offerings and drinking the blessing. The most traditional form is a drinking horn trimmed in metal, or a horn-shaped vessel of glass or metal. Any attractive chalice may serve as second choice.

Every full sacrifice requires several types of offerings. As a bare minimum, clean water can be used for all offerings, but it is best if every power is given a specific gift.

Flour, cornmeal or cakes can offered to the Mother at the opening of the rites. Silver can be offered to the well. This silver may be a special piece of the offerer's magical jewelry or, most preferably, a piece that will later be given permanently to running water. Olive oil, essential oil, or clarified butter can be offered to the Fire. If a candle and censer are used, essential oil can be offered onto charcoal. Ale or other drink can be offered alone to the three Kindreds. For a full offering, ale is given to the ancestors, herbs to the nature spirits, and oil to the gods and goddesses. Enough drink should be present to fill the blessing horn after all offerings have been made.

When offerings are given to the patron deities of the rite, they should be tailored to suit the tastes of those being honored. Drink and oil or incense can always serve, along with flowers and food.

A Simple Devotional

The student assembles the Hallows and may put on her robe or Druidic sign. She makes sure that everything is present, then seats herself before the Hallows. She begins by pausing to find her Peace and Power, then strikes a match and lights the Fire saying:

A Child of the Earth comes to honor the Gods
O blessed Powers of Fire and Water
Light of the Sky, Depth of the Earth
Bring into my Shrine the Divine Fire
Of your wisdom, love and power.
Bring into my Shrine the flow
Of the Power Under the Earth.
The Fire, the Well, the Sacred Tree
Flow and Flame and Grow in me.

The student then invokes the deities and/or spirits in her heart, silently or with such words as she deems proper. She visualizes the forms of the gods and as best he may, seeking a connection with their shining presence. When this link is well established, the student recites the offering, elevating the elements at the proper moments:

I offer my offerings
In the eye of the Mothers who bore me
In the eye of the Fathers who quickened me
In the eye of the Gods and the light of the Fire.
Make me your adopted one,
O Mighty, Noble and Shining Ones

Accept from me (elevate salt)
Salt, that your power preserve and defend me.
(elevate water)
Water that your power cleanse and sustain me.
(elevate incense)
Incense, that your power inspire and delight me.

Bestow upon me in the time of my need
The Love of the Gods
The Wisdom of the Gods
The Power of the Gods
To do in the three worlds as the heroes do in Tir na nOg.

> *Each shade and light*
> *Each day and night*
> *Each hour in blessing*
> *Give to me your spirit*

Anoint self with the salt and water, and pass a hand through the incense. Say:

> *The primal Sea around me*
> *The shining Sky above me*
> *The holy Land beneath me*
> *The Order of the Worlds stands firm*
> *Around me and within my soul.*

Meditation: The student spends a time contemplating the whole pattern of the working.

Upon completing the meditation the dedicant remembers her Peace and Power. She renews the incense if needed, and gives the blessing saying:

> *I offer my praise to the Mother of All.*
> *I offer my praise to the Gods, Dead and Spirits.*
> *May the Three Sacred Kins bring joy to*
> *all beings, and renew the ancient wisdom.*
> *To the Fire, Well and Tree I offer my praise.*
> *May Wisdom, Love and Power*
> *Kindle in all beings,*
> *and renew the ancient wisdom.*
> *To the Earth, Sea, and Sky I offer my praise.*
> *May the ancient wisdom be renewed,*
> *And may all beings know peace, joy and*
> *happiness in all the worlds.*

The student extinguishes the lamp, allowing the incense to burn out.

Brigantia's Celtic Devotions

Morning

Have before you fire and water. Light the fire (such as a candle) with these words:

> *I will kindle the fire this morning*
> *In the presence of the Shining Ones above,*
> *In the presence of the Ancient Ones below,*
> *In the presence of my Noble Kindred all about me.*

Pour out the water from one vessel into another with these words

> *The Three who are in the earth,*
> *The Three who are in the air,*
> *The Three who are in the great pouring sea.*

Dip your fingers into the water and touch your forehead and cheeks with these words:

> *I am bathing my face in pure water,*
> *I am bathing my face in the waters of life,*
> *That I may go clean into this day.*

Pick up the fire and raise it to about eye-level with these words:

> *Strength be in my hands for work,*

> *Wisdom in my speech,*
> *Love in my heart toward all,*
> *And truthful love from all toward me.*

Put on a piece of clothing or of jewelry with these words:

> *Thanks be for my waking,*
> *Thanks be for my rising,*
> *Thanks be for my living,*
> *And for the protection which clothes me.*

Put out the fire with these words:

> *In the Name of the Ancient Ones,*
> *In the Name of the Noble Ones,*
> *In the Name of the Shining Ones,*
> *Go I forth on the path of virtue.*

Pour out the water before leaving the house, preferably onto earth or green things.

Evening Devotions: (to be done just before retiring)

In your sacred space, light a candle in a holder you can carry, or an oil lamp if you prefer. If you wish, sit for a moment with the candle and review your day, what you accomplished, what you are grateful for, what you wish to amend.

When you are ready, go around your home, turn out the lights, and make everything secure, taking the candle or lamp with you. At the door/s of the house, draw a cross over the doorway with the candle, saying:

> *Blessed be this house*
> *From site to stay*
> *From beam to wall*
> *From end to end*
> *From found to summit.*

Envision bands of light encompassing and protecting your home.

Go to your bedroom. Extinguish the lamp or candle with the following words:

> *I am smooring the fire*
> *As Brigid would smoor:*
> *May she bless the fire,*
> *The family, the home;*
> *Brigid the fair to guard us*
> *Till fair day wakes us.*

Settle into bed and repeat the following prayer before sleep:

> *I am lying down tonight*
> *At peace with my kindred,*
> *At peace with my forebears,*
> *At peace with my gods.*
> *The sacred Three*
> *To save, to shield, to surround*
> *The hearth, the family, the home*
> *This night and every night*
> *With the ebb, with the flow.*

Go to sleep.

Basic Druidic Ritual

A Simple Charm of Hallowing

As you begin your Druidic ritual work, you will probably use tools taken from among your possessions, perhaps returning them to common use after each ritual. As you gain experience you will probably want to choose specific items that you find proper and inspiring, and keep these items sacred, set apart from any use except ritual work. It is common to dedicate such items to the work of Druidry through a simple charm of cleansing and empowerment—sometimes called 'hallowing'. This rite is done with any fire and water, though once you have your Hallows it should be done with those tools.

* The object is brought to the shrine, or to the Hallows wherever they are set

* Sprinkle the object with water, and pass it through the smoke or hold it before the fire. Envision the Two Powers flowing over and through it as you say, nine times:

    By the Might of the Waters and the Light of the Fire
    This (object) is made whole and holy!

* Bring the Two Powers into your hands, and take the object into your hands. Speak a blessing proper to the tool, or use a version of this general charm:

    Mighty, Noble and Shining Ones
    Here is my (whatever)
    Offered in service to the work of Druidry.
    Let the Fire be bright in it
    Let the Waters be deep in it
    Let it be as the treasure of wisdom, of love, of power,
    And may it (recite purpose and intention of tool)

* Draw an invoking sign over the object, saying:

    By Fire, Well and Tree
    By Land, sky and Sea
    By Gods, Dead and Sidhe
    By my word and by my will,
    Biodh se amlaidh! (Bee shay awley)

It is best to immediately use the object for its intended purpose, then put it in its place on the shrine.

Part 3

Training the Mind

The Wise know that to control the breath is to control the mind. To begin, sit comfortably, with your spine straight. Your tailbone should be higher than your ankles, your hands resting loosely on your lap or on the arms of your chair. Your eyes may be slightly open, or closed. You then begin a pattern of rhythmic breathing.

Proper breath comes from the diaphragm. When you inhale, your lower abdomen should expand, as though you were pulling air into the bottom of the lungs. Then fill the rest of the lungs, expanding the chest. When the breath is held, do not close the throat. Keep the diaphragm and chest expanded to let the air rest in the lungs. Exhaling reverses the process, emptying the chest then raising the diaphragm by pressing the belly toward the backbone. Again, the breath is held out of the body by the muscles of the chest and belly, not by closing the throat.

Tradition offers several patterns for rhythm of the breath. Many people like the classic 4/4 pattern - in for four beats, hold for four beats, out for four beats, hold for four beats. The speed of the rhythm is up to you. A little practice will allow you to find a pace that is comfortable, neither too slow nor too fast. Some prefer a pattern with shorter holds, perhaps in-4, hold-2, out-4, hold-2.

If you are beginning meditation, your daily practice can be the practice of the Complete Breath, perhaps practiced as a preliminary to your devotions, until it is habitual and comfortable. You will find that it shades naturally into the core techniques of trance and meditation.

A Fire & Water Focusing

To prepare your mind for ritual or meditation, you can use this simple technique with almost any ADF ritual set-up.

Begin a pattern of rhythmic breathing, beginning with three counted breaths. Allow your body to begin to relax as you breathe. Continue the counted breath throughout the exercise.

With your work-hand, place a drop of water on your forehead. Keeping your body relaxed, concentrate on the feel of the water on your skin. Let it fill your awareness.

Focus your gaze on the flame. Let the form and light of the fire be the concentration of your vision.

Take three deep breaths, holding the concentrations on the feeling of the water and the vision of the fire, then say:

Between Fire & Water, I find my balance.

Observe yourself, calmly. Let your concentration always return to the simple focuses, allowing your body to relax. Remember this feeling, and know that you can find it again.

From this start, you can go in several directions:

* Repeat a phrase for yourself, and consider its meaning, while, maintaining your breath and focuses

* Recite an invocation to a Deity or spirit

* Perform a ritual

Simple Pre-Ritual Attunement

1. Stand firm, and take three complete breaths. Find and release tensions in your body as you breathe.
2. Keep your breath rhythmic, and focus on the feeling of your feet touching the ground or floor. For a moment, let your whole attention be on the place where your feet touch the world.
3. Close your eyes, and find the pulse of your heart; in your chest, in your veins, feel the salt flow of your life.
4. Breathe deep, and feel the air flow through you, connecting you with the whole world.
5. Stand firm, on the land. Feel the beating of your heart, and breathe deep. Finally, imagine that a cool white light is shining from your forehead.
6. With your attention focused on these things, open your eyes. Maintain these concentrations, and begin your ritual.

The Two Powers

This is a basic meditation intended to link the Druid's spirit and flesh to the currents of Earth and Sky. It is based on methods that have become known in Pagan work as 'grounding and centering'. All these methods are meant to connect the student to spiritual powers in the cosmos, and to encourage balance in the personal soul. Some form of this technique should precede almost any work of worship or magic.

Later in this book we will give full scripts for 'guided meditation' style calling of the Two Powers. For new students, you can begin with a simpler method:

* Find your seat or your stance, and begin with one of the above exercises.

* Envision dark, rich power that flows like water under your feet. Take three deep, complete breaths and imagine that Underworld Water flowing up into your body

- Envision bright, inspiring power that shines like Fire above your head. Take three deep, complete breaths and imagine that Power of the Heavens shining down into your body.

- Take three deep breaths and envision the Light and the Dark, mingling in your blood, in your breath, in your heart.

- Proceed to your work.

Three Forms of Meditation
By Linda Costello

Meditation holds benefits for mind, body and soul. Research conducted at the stress-reduction clinic at the University of Massachusetts Medical Center in Boston has shown that meditation decreases anxiety, lowers blood pressure, and relieves chronic pain. It can be an important tool for controlling stress and negative emotions, as well as helping the practitioner to become more conscious of connections with the deities.

Meditation is focusing your attention inward, and allowing your mind to settle into stillness. It is withdrawing your consciousness from the outer periphery and bringing it into the inner center. It is the mind's power to hold itself steady. This can be achieved in several different ways. Three common practices are stillness of mind, moving meditation, and guided imagery.

Stillness of Mind

Stillness of Mind doesn't happen overnight. It's something that is achieved through much practice. We all start out with busy minds—we are all immersed in busy lives with many things biding for our attention. We become preoccupied with such things as money, food, job, family, hobby, friends, and we forget to quiet our minds. Eventually, we forget how to quiet our minds.

Through practice, we can slowly regain control, and start training our mind to do our will. To truly master stillness can take years of practice. And although achieving absolute stillness is a lofty goal, just taking the time to try is worthwhile. Any amount of quieting of the mind is beneficial.

A good technique I have found for achieving stillness is to sit quietly and comfortably breathing rhythmically, and just notice your environment. Notice sounds you may hear both close by and in the distance. Notice any smells. Notice what draws your eyes. After awhile, you can notice what thoughts, if any, are flowing through your mind and just watch them flow on by.

In some traditions, no movement at all is allowed. People will be perfectly still for hours, just breathing in and out rhythmically. With practice, you can sit for longer and longer times. Simply sitting quietly like this will lead you more and more towards a serene poise and a quiet mind.

Moving Meditation

Moving meditations can be just as effective, restful and healing as sitting still. Moving meditation is about moving with intention. As you put your attention on how to move, your mind naturally calms.

"Moving meditation allows you to take part in and notice your actions while at the same time maintaining your inner center and calm," says Devya, an African-American certified meditation teacher based in New York. You calm and focus your mind only on the movements you are making, and you block out external distractions. This puts you into a state of mindfulness. With moving meditation, you can bring such mindfulness to any task you are performing, and ordinary events can become profound, sublime experiences.

Guided Imagery

You can also focus your mind inwardly, into a dreamscape that is like a moving meditation, except is happening inside of you, not with your body. Without realizing it, you are focusing your mind in a way that stops the usual mind chatter, and this is what you want to achieve.

An easy way to do this is by using guided imagery. Guided imagery is the process of being asked to focus on selected images to achieve a certain goal. Guided imagery can be used in many ways. You can use guided imagery to aid in relaxation, to increase problem-solving ability and creativity, to promote healing, and to develop desired qualities in yourself.

Guided imagery depends on using the imagination. This can be done in person or by listening to a recording. Imagination is a gateway to creativity, uniqueness, and interpersonal skills, and when the imagination is awakened, worlds open up to you.

When you are using guided imagery, make sure you are in a comfortable and safe place, free from distraction. You want to be able to immerse yourself in your inner world of imagination to achieve optimal results.

Meditation takes many forms, but ultimately achieves the same results—a quieter mind, a greater mindfulness, and increased awareness. Try it. You'll like it.

Some resources used:

Websites

- http://www.meditationsociety.com/index.html
- http://findarticles.com/p/articles/mi_m1264/is_12_31/ai_72434997
- http://psychcentral.com/lib/2006/guided-visualization-a-way-to-relax-reduce-stress-and-more/
- http://www.meditation.com/MeditationPractice.html

Books

- Wood, Ernest; Concentration, An Approach to Meditation

Part 4

Attunement to Nature & the Kindreds

The heart of the work of Druidry can be seen and known in nature. There is no doubt that our work requires intellectual effort, study and training of the mind. In the end, all of those skills only allow us to relate more deeply to the reality of the physical world. Through understanding of nature–its processes, forms and wonders, we come to understand the meaning and means of the Otherworld and the Spirits. Simply put, study, ritual and meditative work must always be balanced with experiences of the real presence of the natural world. Of course, Indo-European Paganism was strongly 'artificial'. That is, the old ways valued the human ability to shape the things of nature into things useful to humankind. Much of the symbolism of Pagan ways is concerned with human efforts to gain good from the indifferent, even hostile environment.

When a mortal clan enters a new land, they must begin by comprehending the wilderness. They must approach and ally with the Gods and Goddesses of the forest, and win a place in which to carve out their lives. Modern Pagans face a different challenge. Most of us come from societies cut off, by distance and by layers of technology, from wilderness, and even from the common processes of nature. We live in boxes many feet above the ground, eat packaged food, drink bottled water. Our cities and farms were built without regard for the spirits of place - for the intrinsic holiness of the land.

As Paganism re-awakens in our modern lands, we can make it part of our work to restore the relationship between mortals and the land. We can go to the woods, and absorb the patterns and forms of the wild. We can become aware of the natural places even in our own cities and suburbs. We can begin re-enchanting the landscape of our homes - our wells and pools, our crossroads and hilltops. All of that begins by getting out of our living-rooms and into the natural world.

The Basics

Your relation to the natural world should be both practical and spiritual. Practically, you should make it your business to learn the facts about your landscape. Learn the trees and herbs, the animals and birds, the stones and soil most common to your region. Learn how water flows through your land, where the weather comes from, and what crops come from farms and gardens.

In the same way, we encourage you to consider yourself an active defender of the land on which you live and worship. Human inattention and greed are threatening the World Order - upsetting the balances that sustain our lives and those of our nonhuman co-dwellers on Earth. As people who consider the land to be part of our holy ways, we should make it our business to protect it from poison and destruction.

Here are some study questions to help you understand your land:

* What is the source of your drinking water? What rivers make up your watershed?
* What are the prevailing winds? What are the major influences on your local clouds, rain and storms?
* What is the composition of your soil? Is it acid or alkali? What are the major crops grown in your region?
* Identify 5 species of trees in your area. Then, learn 4 more!
* Identify 5 herbs for health in your area. Then, learn 4 more!
* Identify 5 species of birds common to your area, and 5 species of wild animal.
* Know the three major sources of air and water pollution in your area.
* Know how your area deals with trash and garbage. Consider recycling and/or composting.
* Learn about environmental action groups in your area; consider joining and/or working with one or more.

Opening Your Spirit to the Land

It is vital for you to make a true and deep contact with the forms and processes of nature. One way to approach that is to use basic trance to open your self to those patterns. While it is good to actually leave the city when possible, it is not necessary to go deep into the wild to do this work. Every city has park land, back yards, even decorative trees that allow contact with forms not shaped by humankind.

When you have a little skill in finding your Peace and Power, go out to a place where you can sit quietly on the grass or a low bench or mat. If you can find a place where more than one kind of natural form occurs–trees, herbs, beasts, stones, streams–then that is best. Seat yourself as comfortably as possible and begin your pattern of rhythmic breathing.

Sitting with your eyes closed, find the rhythm of your breath, and work one of the basic mental exercises. After a while allow yourself to begin to listen to the sounds around you. Let those sounds enter your mind and flow through you, hearing all but holding to nothing. The goal is to keep your mental balance and calm no matter the input. When you wish, open your eyes. Let the sights of the natural world move through your mind. Allow your eye to flow over the forms of the natural world, even linger to look closely. But when any thought or image grasps or holds the attention, return to counting the breath and let eye and mind move on. The goal is to sit in silence, your mind transparent to the reality of the woodland, offering no obstacle to the flow of nature's sights and sounds.

The final phase of this work is to stand and walk while maintaining the 'open eye'. When this can be managed with a minimal number of breaks, you will have a skill that can help you in every part of your life from labor's drudgery to the sublime moments of vision and magic.

If you wish, your efforts to become aware of the Spirits in any specific place can be expressed in a spoken charm or prayer. When you have felt welcomed in any natural place it is always good to give a small offering, perhaps spilling a little drink upon the ground, and saying:

> *The world is in me, and I am in the world*
> *The Spirit in me is the Spirit in the world.*
> *To you, place of beauty, place of honor,*
> *To you (name and describe place)*
> *I bring this offering in peace.*
> *From the Deep in me to the Deep in you*
> *From my Fire to your Fire*
> *A gift of honor, a gift of worship*
> *In hope of your welcome*
> *That there be peace between us*
> *In all things*
> *Be it so!*

The Spirits in the Land

The work of Druidry is about building relationships between mortals and the Spirits. We seek to reach out to the Spirits whether of our land, or of our folk. In order to comprehend the vast families of the Gods and the Non-Gods, we think of them in the categories which we call the Three Kindreds.

As you begin the work of Druid ritual and study, you can begin to seek an understanding of each of these groups of Spirits. Your readings in mythology and Pagan culture should give you the basic concepts of the nature of the Deities, the Dead and the Land-Spirits. However, it is proper to look to the land itself to find out how the God/desses and Spirits are present in your region.

The Shining Ones

The Divine Ones, the Gods and Goddesses, are those beings mightiest among all the Spirits. As you study the culture and religion of an ancient people, it is usually the Shining Ones who stand out–who are most apparent. Their help and love, their power and beauty, have caused them to be remembered even as other aspects of Pagan cultures are forgotten.

In any region there are places that are unique, natural features that command the attention and respect of the communities near them. In many places, especially in the U.S., these places have been made part of public parks and preserves. These can be reached easily by car or on foot. In other cases important natural features, such as mountains, stones or caves, are found outside the city, in wild places.

These notable natural places are proper for seeking contacts with the Shining Ones. It is helpful to go to these sites, taking with you a collection of the tales of the God/desses of your choice of culture. There you can sit and read a key tale or two–perhaps even reading aloud–while sitting in communion with the site. You might choose to imagine the form or presence of one or more of the Deities in the natural setting, and make a small offering, perhaps of precious metal or stones, or whatever is proper for those Powers that you seek.

In attuning to the Gods and Goddesses, two major land features are often central. First determine what the major river and/or source of drinking water is for your region. If you can, find the source and headwaters for the river, and make an effort to reach them. At your local waterside you should contemplate the Goddesses, seeking to attune yourself to the Lady of the Land.

Secondly, determine where the highest point is in your region. Ancient Indo-European religion always looked to the high places to find the Shining Ones, and the principle applies today as well. On the high places you can call out to all the Shining Ones, and especially to the Gods of sky, of storm and of the sun.

In all such places it is proper to attune to the Gods and Goddesses. Go with an open heart, make a simple offering, and listen with your spirit to the land.

The Mighty Dead

The Ancestors, the Dead of the Clans of Mortals are our own kin and folk in the Otherworld. The tales and traditions of Pagan cultures are full of the heroes–men and women–of the Old Ways. These great mortal lives stand as an example to the living of cultural virtues and the power of the Spirits. The heroes are the link between present mortal lives and the human past.

Just as important as the great ones of any tribe are the past members of one's own clan. Grandmothers and grandfathers, one's own forbearers, are worthy of veneration. Cultures with strong traditions of ancestor worship place great importance on the relationship between the living and the Dead. The Mighty Dead have vision and magic beyond those of mortals, and can have great influence over the lives of their descendants. So it is proper for us to give love, reverence and offerings to the spirits of our own Beloved Dead.

The Dead are honored in our local environment in several ways. Most common are the cemeteries used by modern religions and civic governments. While many of these are filled with very un-Pagan symbols and sentiments, they can also have some inspiring statuary and natural places. In cemeteries we sometimes find great trees, glens of flowers, and images of classical beauty.

Most cities also have a variety of civic, nonreligious, monuments. We remember those dead in war, and those who fell in service to the culture in various causes. Finding these places brings us into contact with our urban environment, and may be enshrined in green places amidst the concrete and glass. These places can provide a sense of contact with the history of local culture, a thing always sacred to Pagan ways.

In these places you can make contacts with the green places in our cities, and with the spirits of the mighty and beloved Dead. Go to these places and read the tales of the legendary heroes of your chosen Pagan culture. Be aware also of the stories of famous heroes of your region, and learn the tales of the Dead of your own families. Take with you offerings of food and drink, make your offerings in love and reverence, and open your heart to the voices of the Ancestors.

The Noble Spirits

Throughout the worlds, in every place, there are many Tribes of Spirits. Beings of wonderful diversity, some beautiful, some hideous, the Noble Spirits are beings who serve the Gods in maintaining the Order of the Worlds. Some dwell in lonely places apart from company, keeping a pool or stone or tree as their domain. Others dwell together in glittering courts, keeping their revels and feasts. These beings are neither Gods nor Dead. They may rightly be considered as lesser relations of the Deities, assigned by them to hold the natural world in proper order.

The Gods are our allies, the Dead our kin, but the Spirits are, in many ways, quite separate from us. They are the Other, and as such they are not automatically our allies and friends. In many tales they are the enemies of humankind, or must be carefully placated. When we approach these spirits today, we approach nature in the wild, the untamed reality that is the basis of all tame life.

Yet we also see that some of the Spirits choose to work for, or with, mortals, especially for the fertility of the land. So we know that they can be our allies as well, if we approach them with respect.

When we seek contact with the Nobles we seek places wild and tangled, untouched as much as possible by human work. Go out from the cities and parklands and fields, or find places within them overgrown and untended. If you keep a yard or field as your own, it might be good to leave a small section of it completely untended, as a place in which the Nobles can feel welcome and honored. In many places there are patches of relative wilderness even in habited places. Look closely in you own area, but remember to get out of the city and the farmland and into the real wilderness.

Even in cities the Nobles watch and ward, keeping the lives of the nonhuman Kins. There may even be a greater Lord or Lady, keeping a court. But it is in the wilder places that you may come to glimpse the greater Spirits, the Wild Powers. When you go to seek them and make your offerings, go with care. Be certain to be fully prepared for the reality of the wilderness, and go with the greatest respect both for the wild land, and for the Spirits that you seek.

These first efforts to attune to the land and the spirits are an opportunity to begin simple ritual. We provide, below, a very simple approach to greeting the spirits in a natural place. It requires a minimum of tools and allows attention to be focused on the natural locale.

The skills of the basic nature attunement, the application of 'open-ness' type meditation to the perceptions of a natural environment, are central to this work. While there is value in using the imagination to construct forms for the Spirits, it is perhaps better to begin by simply offering worship, then opening your eyes, ears and heart to the real presences of the land. Expect nothing at this stage, or expect everything; but set aside your expectations and open to your senses. Then, when vision comes, it will be ensouled by the reality of the land.

It is also possible, and useful, to approach the land and the spirits with no ceremony at all. Simply working the open-eyed meditation in various settings will go some way toward making strong natural contacts. The Druid's way is, however, a way of ritual, and greater results are likely to come from even simple ritual work.

Part 5

Simple Omens for Ritual

One of the core skills of the Druid's art is divination—the use of magic to discover that which is unknown. We divine to determine what is unseen in the present and past, and what the pattern of Dan may hold for our future. In Druidic ritual we also often divine to determine whether the spirits are pleased with our work, whether our offerings have been accepted, whether our work is headed for a good outcome, and what kind of power is being offered by the spirits.

In this work we will not attempt to teach the sort of divination that allows us to do complex 'readings'. While the simple techniques given here can be used for that sort of 'telling', there are many books from which you can better gain those skills. Here we will address methods of taking the sorts of simpler omens that are required for ritual work.

Appendix E has charts with basic correspondences for both Runes and Ogham. For more in-depth information about these two systems, please see the Recommended Reading Lists in Appendix A under "Ogham and Runes".

Sortilege

Sortilege is the taking of omens by the drawing of lots. One takes a bag or bowl of symbols on identical pieces of wood or stone, or on a deck of cards, and randomly draws a few symbols. The meanings of those symbols provide the omen or answer to an inquiry.

In order to divine by sortilege you will need to draw the letters of the alphabet or symbol system which you are using on identical lots. There is a traditional account that suggests that the lots should be prepared fresh each time you wish to take an omen. There is value in that approach but practicality suggests the creation of a permanent, personal set of divination lots. This chapter will focus on two traditional alphabets—the Ogham and the Runes.

The Ogham

The Ogham alphabet originated in Ireland in the first few centuries of the common era. It was used primarily as a simple way of carving inscriptions on grave and memorial stones and border markers. In later Irish lore the Ogham becomes a kind of bardic and poetic code, which modern Celtic Pagans have taken up as a set of symbols for divination and spell-work. The Ogham is commonly thought of as the 'alphabet of trees'. The most famous of the Ogham lists gives ancient tree-names for each of the letters. The Irish Ogham lists go on to list Oghams of birds, ships, cities and many other kinds.

Ogham lots might best be made of bits of square dowel. We can imagine a perfect set made with each dowel cut from the proper sort of wood. This is a worthwhile long-term project, but to get started you will probably need to use commercial dowel. A square dowel allows you to use one corner as the centerline of the Ogham letter. That leaves two sides on which you might write the Irish and English names of the tree-letter.

Here we offer the Tree Ogham with simple divinatory meanings to enable you to begin taking simple omens immediately. The focus of this work does not allow us to spend as much time on the meaning and use of the Oghams as it deserves. The Ogham is one of the most systematic views we have of the early Celtic mind—it is a link to the Celtic core of the magic we seek.

The Runes

The Runes are the magical alphabet of the Norse peoples, a Germanic folks with close blood and cultural ties to the Celts. Both on the European continent and in the British Isles, Norse clans mingled with Celts, to the enrichment of both peoples. The Runes are not a Celtic system, but their meanings and context so closely match those of Celtic cultures that they can properly be a part of the Celtic sorcerer's tools.

Rune lots can be made of wooden disks, or of disks of a tree-branch, carefully cut to even thickness and size. Each disk is then graven with one Rune. The most traditional means is to actually carve the Rune into the wood, then to stain it red.

Again, there are many resources for learning the Runes. If they call to you, there are many references available. Here we will offer only a simple chart of names and divinatory meanings.

Whether making Ogham or runic lots, the wood should be cut to size, and then purified with the Fire and Water Hallowing charm, along with any ink, paint or tool that you mean to use. The process of inscribing the symbols will place your energy into them, so do not cleanse and purify them after they have been carved. Your omen tool should be kept on your shrine and treated as an important hallow.

Seeking an Omen by Sortilege

The very simplest method of drawing an omen by sortilege is to draw a single lot. The symbol is then interpreted in light of the nature of the work at hand. The most reliably attested traditional method of sortilege involves drawing three lots. Depending on the apparent answer in the first three symbols, two more qualifying or clarifying questions may be asked.

In a public rite of worship the omen-question often: 'What blessings do the spirits offer us in return for our offerings.' Some draw one lot each for each of the Kindreds, asking what blessings come from the Gods, Dead and Spirit. Some Groves use a slightly more complex set of questions, such as: 'Is the offering accepted?', 'What blessing do you offer?', 'What advice do you give?'. It is good to begin simply, asking after the blessing offered.

Neither Ogham nor Runes are likely to produce a simple yes or no answer. If the symbols plainly agree with the nature of the work at hand, the omen can be considered a good one, the answer a 'yes'. If it is plainly opposed to the work then the omen may be considered bad, or the answer a 'no'.

If you receive a bad omen you may choose to ask additional questions. A series of yes/no or qualitative questions may reveal how you can gain the goal you seek. If you receive a bad omen at a key point in ritual you will have the choice to attempt to improve the omen through additional sacrifices or other efforts, to shut down the rite and await a more auspicious day, or to go forward with the working despite the omens.

A Simple Method of Taking an Omen by Lot

Be seated at your hallows, and have your bag or bowl of symbol-lots, and a white cloth on which to lay the omen. If you need to you may have a simple book or guide to the meaning of the signs.

Pause for a moment and remember your Center and your Power. Open your mind to the whole pattern of the rite within which you are divining.

* Take up the bowl or bag, and shake or stir the lots, shuffling them well. If you wish you might recite a simple charm as you do, such as:

> *Wisdom seek I in these signs,*
> *That seeing and knowing be mine.*
> *Mighty, Noble and Shining Ones, tell me I ask,*
> *(state question.)*

* Draw three lots, one at a time. As you draw each lot, identify it, speak its name aloud and recite aloud two or three key words of its meaning.

* Lay all three lots in a row before you. Pause for a moment, and, from your own Stillness, consider the meaning of the three symbols you have been given. This is the answer to your query.

Some like to leave the omen layed-out before the Hallows while the Blessing is received, some like to pack them away again. It can be useful to write the omen down immediately.

Part 6

The Very Basics of Ritual

Human society has, to our knowledge, always been filled with ritual. From home to temple to village square to national capitol, ritual brings people together to focus on goals that transcend the physical world, goals based on symbolism and spiritual things. Ritual is so basic to human life that it has seldom been clearly defined. Social science has spent some effort to understand ritual, but there is only limited agreement in academic circles. For the purposes of this discussion, we will focus on ritual as it is used to serve spiritual or religious needs.

We can define ritual, for our purposes, as an intentional series of acts, formulated and repeated. Some writers have included rote or merely repetitive acts in the definition of ritual. For the purposes of our work we will use the word only to refer to those repeated patterns which are deliberately devised and intentionally performed.

Most ritual is intended to express a spiritual reality in the physical and social realms. Love or honor, justice or generosity, spiritual principles and the Gods and Spirits are the sorts of non-material things for which ritual has been created. Humans have always recognized that spiritual things make their mark in the material world. This reflection of the spiritual and the material—'as above, so below, and as below, so above'—produces what tradition has called 'correspondences' linking herbs and stars and stones and symbols with spiritual forces and beings. In nature this can be as simple as golden things being considered solar and silver things, lunar, but the symbolism has become subtle and complex over the centuries. In the same way, spiritual forces produce symbols and ideas in the human mind, inspiring art and music that uplifts us, in turn. Ritual brings all these things together in an artful pattern that makes a concentration of symbols of spiritual things and encourages communication between humankind and the Gods.

The ancients described ritual as made up of 'things done and things said'. This remains entirely true—almost every ritual contains these things. In our time we add a third category. For us, religious ritual consists of 'things done, 'things said' and 'things thought'. The words and actions of a well-done ritual ought to naturally lead our thoughts to the sacred, but the ability to deliberately guide thought and imagination during ritual is as valuable as a steady hand and a clear voice.

Ritual work is a skill. It is easy to learn the basics, and to work simple rites at home for the work of your own spirituality. This guide offers well-developed rites, fully scripted and with instructions for the gestures and actions of the rite. Within these ready-to-work rites you will begin to learn to direct your thought and imagination along with your voice and body. From there we offer more complex patterns, leading to skill in a simple but complete performance of our Druidic Order of Ritual. As a student of music proceeds from simple exercises to more complex pieces, just so ritual skill grows from beginning figures to more detailed patterns of working.

So, to summarize:

1. Ritual is repeated, intentional action, especially that which concerns symbolic or spiritual things.
2. Ritual is a combination of Things Done, Things Said, and Things Thought.
3. Every human art may be employed in ritual. Graphic art, sculpture and craft, poetry, music and song, and rhetoric are used individually or in combinations.
4. Ritual is a skill that anyone can learn, through practice. Everyone begins with simple forms and grows into deeper practice.

Basics of Ritual

Intention

Every ritual must have a specific purpose. At the simplest level this can always run along the lines of 'to worship and attune with the Gods and Spirits' or 'to strengthen and empower my own spirit' Our ritual calendar provides a regular round of seasonal intentions in the Eight High Days. In them we work the whole round of the life of the land, from seed to shoot to bloom to fruit, and then the harvest. Shrine work in the home helps us build a web of relationship with those Gods and Spirits who call us, or are called. In more specific personal work we might work ritual for healing, seership, to bless a life with prosperity, awaken inspiration or any of the traditional 'magical' goals. The important point is to always be clear in your intention when you enter ritual.

Pattern

Most rituals are based around and within a symbolic pattern or map of the spiritual powers. The basic pattern of ritual will determine the nature and arrangement of the physical symbolic objects used, as well as a great deal of the speech. The most famous NeoPagan ritual pattern is the Wiccan Circle, with the 'Four Elements' arranged in the quarters. Our Druidic rites are based in a different map, one that uses sets of three symbols, arranged in 'Triads'. Our Druidry has grown some amount of consensus on the 'cosmology'—the map of the spiritual worlds—that we use in our rites, though there is some variance based on local cultural preferences.

Timing

Tradition teaches us to work our rituals within the cycles of nature. The High Rites of the seasonal feasts keep us in tune with the great cycles of the year, of sun and earth. Other rites, especially those for 'magical' intentions are best timed with the waxing and waning of the moon. The twilight hours of Dusk and Dawn hold special enchantment. When in doubt simple rites, such as the Self-Blessing, should be worked at the moon's first quarter at sunset.

Tools

A ritual is a symbolic pattern, which uses words, ideas and physical symbols. Some physical things in ritual are occasional—seasonal or intentional objects used only in specific rites. The key ritual objects—the 'tools' of the ritual trade that you will use in most formal rites regardless of intention, are made and kept with much more care.

In Our Druidic ritual we have come to build our ritual patterns around three key tools. Ritual water is kept in a vessel, often a cauldron, which we call the 'Well'. Live fire is central to Pagan ritual. A metal vessel or tray holds the 'Fire', even if it is only a few candles and a holder for incense. The third key tool represents both the sacred center and the whole Order of the Worlds. A simple symbolic pillar or an image of a tall tree—just large enough to stand well above the Fire and Well—can serve as a ritual 'Tree' This symbol has several cultural variations. Some might prefer an actual tree-shaped symbol, while others might prefer a tall stone, or a symbol of the World Mountain. In any case, these three symbols are commonly referred to as the 'Fire, Well & Tree'.

These symbols are arranged together to create the working center of most of our Druidic rituals. Often they are placed directly on the floor or earth, or on a cloth upon it. For solo rites they might be arranged on a table. The Fire Well & Tree—sometimes called the 'Hallows' of the rite—are the 'altar' of the ritual, whether they are on a table or just arranged on the ground.

There are several kinds of tools we might call secondary Druidic tools. You may wish to make or obtain a robe, tunic or cloak, which you reserve for ritual wear only. Many people choose a specific piece of jewelry—a ring, torc or symbolic pendant, which they wear only for ritual. Whether your ritual 'garb' is complex or minimal, it is useful to have some symbol of your Druidic work which you dedicate to ritual occasions.

Our rituals usually involve receiving a blessing by drinking from a cup or horn. If you wish you might choose a special cup or vessel that is kept sacred to the blessing. This can become a subtle symbol of your own spirit, which receives and integrates the Blessing of the Powers.

In addition to the Well, you may need a separate bowl to receive offerings of ale, grain etc. This Offering Bowl can be a kind of secondary tool related to the Well, placed next to it in the Hallows for indoor rites. When such a bowl is used, the offerings are taken outside as soon as possible and given to a tree or opening in the ground.

Tradition tells us that the very best tools are those made skillfully by your own hand. Tradition isn't wrong, and there is great satisfaction in learning artisans' skills in order to make your own sacred things. There is also no harm in purchasing fine tools, though if you can buy them from other Pagans so much the better. However there is no reason not to begin by simply 'making do', with objects readily available at home. As you work your first rituals, feel free to keep it simple—a bowl of Water can serve as the Well, three candles and an incense burner can be your Fire, and a shapely branch in a candle-holder can serve as your Tree. By beginning simply you will become familiar with the ritual and the use of the tools, and when the right objects present themselves, you'll recognize them.

Mind and Spirit

In ancient days the symbolic power of ancient places, of holy objects and traditional words, would have carried the minds of the villagers into the altered states of awareness that allow contact with the Otherworlds. In our day, when we must construct our holy symbols for ourselves, it is important to deliberately induce the proper states of mind. The basic state of awareness we seek for our Druidic rituals is sometimes called 'Stillness and Strength', or 'Center and Power'. First we seek a place of calm poise, behind the chatter of our daily mind. Then we seek a connection to the spiritual energies of the cosmos. In common with many Pagan systems we draw on the energies of Earth and Sky to strengthen our spirits.

Words & Scripts

Well structured words are a powerful enhancement to ritual. On the other hand, words spoken simply and clearly from the moment's inspiration have great strength as well. The ancient Druids both memorized large bodies of poetry and lore, and learned to compose beautiful words ex tempore.

As you begin ritual work you should feel free to use printed 'scripts'. There is no reason not to begin by reading rites directly from this book. There is also value in writing out the text, or typing it in, and arranging the text in a large, easy-to-read format. The creation of a personal book of rites is an old tradition that still has a great deal of value.

There is an art to reading ritual scripts aloud in a meaningful and effective way. Read the rite often and carefully as you prepare. Be sure you have considered the meaning and context of each phrase. It is a good idea to practice reading the words aloud as 'rehearsal', to find the pace and phrasing that works for you.

Memorization is, of course, a traditional Druidic practice. It is always good to memorize the rites you perform. Memorization and regular practice are the best way to make a ritual your own. However, attempting a memorized rite without being entirely sure of yourself can be a distraction, and losing track of your words can end in an aborted effort. In early work you should keep a text of the rite near, and feel comfortable in referring to it at need.

When you work a ritual written by someone else, you are, to a certain extent, entering into a symbolic world other than your very own. In ancient times this was a world defined by tradition and tribal myth and culture, and most ritualists would have grown up inside the symbolism in which they worked. In our time we are re-inventing our Pagan symbolism and concepts. When we work a scripted ritual we must set aside our critical faculty and seek to experience the symbolic world inherent in the ritual's pattern and words. When you choose to allow your thoughts and feelings to be guided by the meaning of the words and symbols, you will get the most out of any rite. In Our Druidry we have a basic symbolism and cosmology that infuses most of our rites. When you choose to work in our Order of Ritual, you will find yourself in familiar territory with almost any ADF script.

ADF ritual has always been designed in a set of 'modules' or steps: Opening Prayers, Gate Opening, Triad Invocations, etc. In many ways the best approach to ritual without paper scripts is to know the order of ritual outline in detail, and have a clear understanding of the intention and practice for each step. You can then say simple (or intricate), proper words for the steps, without need for a script. As you practice, you will gather bits of 'traditional' ADF ritual speech, some used in many Groves, which can be used in your unscripted rites. Most rituals will contain special sections unique to the intention of the rite, such as the seasonal customs in a High day rite. Even if you become used to working personal rites without a script you might use a script for these special sections of a rite. Memorization, extemporization and scripts can all work together in any ritual.

Working Ritual

Preparation

The best way to feel secure about working a ritual is to be properly prepared. Be certain that you have the full list of tools, offerings and items that the rite calls for. Be certain that you understand the intention of the rite, and have some knowledge of the Gods and Spirits involved. Decide when and where you will work, and as you approach the hour of the rite, make sure that the space is clean and ordered, with enough room for your set-up. Try to set aside at least two hours before you intend to begin. During this time you should bathe, study the ritual, and finish your physical set-up, making sure all the tools and offerings are in place.

Set-Up

Our Druidic ritual is built around the Triple Center—the Well (Earth Power, Underworld), the Fire (Sky Power, Heavens) and the Tree (Middle World, Crossroads). These Three Hallows (as they are sometimes called) are arranged in the center of the ritual working space. If you wish to work seated you will arrange the Hallows so that they are in easy reach of your seat. Often it is best to place the Fire closest to you, but some rites may call for a greater number of offerings to be made into a bowl. Those who can comfortably sit cross-legged might be able to set their Fire right on the earth, though it also very traditional to be raised above ground level.

Choose your spot, and decide whether you will work on the ground or floor, perhaps with cloth large enough for you to sit upon, with the Hallows arranged on it as well. If you are more comfortable on a chair, you might arrange the rite on a small table-top before you. Of course, whenever you can get outside, you should consider taking the opportunity. In such cases you may be able to build an actual Fire, whether on the ground or in an iron cauldron, or a barbecue, etc—always a fine enhancement.

Place your Three Hallows in a way that suggests a balanced center. Some Druids like an 'axis' arrangement with the tall Tree in the back, and the raised Fire and low Well before it. Others prefer a more triangular arrangement. The most traditional orientation is to sit with your back to the west, facing east over the central symbols. Some Northern traditions prefer to face the Pole Star, back to the south.

Most rituals will require additional objects, symbols and offerings. You will need offerings for the Earth Mother, Gatekeeper, and Three Kindreds, at least, and some rites require additional offerings. In simple cases you might make offerings of incense to all, but more detailed offerings are quite appropriate. Our rituals usually involve receiving a blessing by drinking from a cup or horn. You will need drink to fill the vessel. If you wish you might choose a special cup or vessel that is kept sacred to the blessing. This is sometimes considered a fourth hallow, one that is sacred to your own spirit, and to the blessing of the Powers upon it.

High Day rites may call for special seasonal symbols—eggs for spring, black ribbons for Samhain, etc. Each High Day rite is worked under the special blessing of one or more Deities, and/or the Dead or Spirits. You may wish to use images of the Deities, or symbolic objects—a cauldron for the Dagda, a raven for Odin. While a variety of well-made statues are available you can also find many good images in various decks of oracle cards, or use natural things—stones, pinecones, etc.

The general goal in setting up a ritual is to make a central display of the symbols that express the intention of the rite, around and with the Hallows. This arrangement should be attractive to you, while remaining precise to the intention. Make sure that the area has enough light—extra candles are always good. The offerings and other 'disposables' of the rite can be set to one side in a place ready to hand. As you approach the time for the ritual, take a final moment to review each of the steps of the rite, and be certain that each object called for by the script is available—as the old Druid says "Go count your offerings."

The Mind and Body in Ritual

Ritual is a method of connecting the mortal mind and spirit with the immortal beings and impersonal powers of the spiritual worlds. All of the material symbolism, patterns, poetry and gestures are intended to create, and are energized by, altered states of awareness. The distractions and obsessions of mundane life and work must be exchanged for a strong focus on spiritual things. This work of focus is greatly enhanced by the skilled control of attention, relaxation and visualization. We use specific techniques of managing attention and mental contents to create the states of mind that support spiritual experience. Technically, this is called using 'trance' by modern consciousness researchers, and by many Pagans. Don't confuse this technical meaning with ideas of trance as unconsciousness or reduced awareness.

The essential mental state for spiritual ritual is a combination of physical relaxation, concentrated attention and the suspension of immediate criticism. This state has been called 'basic trance', and is the base on which other intentional mental states are built. In our work we sometimes refer to it as 'finding stillness', or as the (Druid's) Peace. It allows us to set aside, for a time, the emotional involvements and mental chatter of daily awareness. The advice of ancient teachers agrees that the voices of the spiritual world are heard more clearly when the robotic chatter of the daily mind is bypassed.

Our rites regularly use a second technique. Using visualization and intention, we open ourselves to the impersonal spiritual powers of the Underworld and the Heavens. This is often done through some variation of the well-known Pagan 'Tree meditation'—roots below and sun above—but there are many other techniques. This awareness of power flowing in the self creates a connection between the personal spirit and the web of energies in the greater spiritual world. We sometimes call this 'grounding and centering' or 'finding one's Power'.

In working ritual, you will usually begin any working by taking a few minutes to find this basic mental poise. As you gain experience you will find yourself automatically maintaining the proper states of awareness throughout the ritual. When you are learning, you may find it difficult to identify, induce or maintain your relaxed, concentrated awareness during ritual. Do the exercises given, and work your way through the rite. You should pause regularly throughout the ritual to be sure that your Peace and Power are maintained and strengthened. Even if you do not begin the rite in a well-focused state of mind, you may find that it comes to you in the course of the work.

Physical Poise and Voice

Ritual involves the whole self. While it is focused on the spiritual, ritual is a physical act. To work ritual you must use your body and voice together in a deliberate, focused way. The three elements of body-use in ritual are balance, relaxation and movement.

Relaxation relieves the body of habitual tension and discomfort. Tension in the body disrupts the flow of power, and distracts the mind. Ritual should always be done from a place of physical balance and poise. A straight spine, firm footing, and a supple stance bring focus and flexibility to the mind. Ritual requires movement, and every movement and gesture in ritual space should serve a specific symbolic purpose. Fidgeting, or any aimless or thoughtless movement only dissipates some of the rite's energy.

Spoken words are another of the keys to ritual. Until an intention is expressed in words it remains half-formed, its potential unrealized. Even in solitary ritual it is best that words be spoken aloud. You will need to find a ritual voice that seems powerful and sustainable. You should avoid overly dramatic exaggeration, artificial loudness or foreign accents. If you absolutely must try to conceal your rituals you might choose to speak in a whisper or low voice. Otherwise you should seek a speaking voice that is clear, easily heard and satisfying.

Will and Work–Ending the Rite

The ancients said that the opening and closing of ritual are like the two wheels of a chariot, they must be balanced in order to accomplish the goal. When you choose to work spiritual ritual, you enter into a promise with the Gods and Spirits. Each rite is a complete event—opening, intention and closing. Never approach the close of ritual in a rush, or view it as mere clean-up. Whenever you kindle sacred Fire you should make certain to see the work through to a proper end. Any time you make a Grove and open a Gate, the work is your responsibility. Never light a Fire that you cannot tend, never open a gate that you do not close.

A Solitary Self-Blessing Rite

You should have a complete set of Hallows (even if it's improvised), and a good, comfortable seat placed before them, located so that you can reach all sections of the work area. Materials Needed: Small bell, fire-pot or candle & censer with incense (the Fire), cauldron with blessed water (the Well), world tree, mountain or gate symbol or wand or staff set up as a pillar (the Tree), a horn or cup for pouring and drinking, an offering bowl before the Fire if the rite is indoors, offerings (corn meal, silver, olive oil or essential oil, or incense) ale, fruit juice or water for offering and drinking, and a tool with which to take an omen.

The oil might be kept in a vial, from which small offerings are poured, but it is slightly more traditional to use a bowl of oil and a spoon or small ladle to give it to the fire. If one uses incense, then powdered incense spooned on to charcoal gives the same feel. Non-burnable offerings are made into the offering bowl, which is emptied into earth after the rite.

[1] Give nine knells on a bell, then raise hands to the sky, and say:

I am here to honor the gods, and to bless myself in the Old Way. Be with me, Oh Shining Ones, in my working; forgive any errors, and grant me, I pray, your blessing.

[2] Offer a pinch of corn meal onto the ground, saying:

Earth Mother, I am your child. Mother of all I pray you bless and uphold my rite, as you uphold the whole world. Earth Mother, accept my sacrifice!

[3] Place your hands on your heart and open to the light of inspiration, saying:

Sky Father, Fire of Inspiration, attend the shrine of my soul. Quicken my tongue that I may work this rite in beauty.

[4] State the purpose of the rite, saying:

I have come to do as the wise ancients did, to make offering to the powers and to bless my body, my mind and my spirit with the blessings of the Gods and Spirits. As our forebears did, so do I do now, and so may my descendants do after me.

I seek the blessing of the Ancestors, of the Landspirits, and of the Shining Gods and Goddesses. I seek to be cleansed of ill, and filled with the fire and water of the ancient blessing, that I may grow in health, and wealth and wisdom, in wisdom, love and power, in service to the spirits, and to the folk and to my own being. To those ends, I will hallow this sacred Grove.

[5] Offer silver into the cauldron, saying:

In the deeps flow the waters of wisdom. Sacred well, flow within me.

[6] Make an offering to the Fire, saying:

I feed the sacred fire in wisdom, love and power. Sacred fire, burn within me.

[7] Sprinkle and cense the world-tree, wand or self, saying:

From the deeps to the heights spans the world-tree. Sacred tree, grow within me.

[8] Sprinkle everything with sacred water, and cense all with incense from the Fire; see the Powers flowing in the whole Shrine turning away ill, repeating three times:

By the might of the Water and the light of the Fire, this Grove is made whole and holy

[9] Spread your hands, and encompass the whole shrine in your awareness, saying:

Let the sea not rise, and all ill turn away.
Let the sky not fall and all ill turn away.
Let the land hold firm and all ill turn away.

[10] Contemplate the three worlds and the Shrine, saying:

The Fire, the Well, the Sacred Tree, flow and flame and grow in me!
In Land, Sea, and Sky, below and on high! Thus is the Sacred Grove claimed and hallowed. So be it!

[11] Offer oil or incense to the fire, saying:

I make this offering to the Keeper of the Gates.
Gatekeeper, Lord of the Between, Keeper of Roads and
Opener of Ways, join your magic with mine
to guard and ward the gate of this working.
Gatekeeper, accept my sacrifice!

[12] Make a deosil triskel or spiral over the Fire, saying:

In every place where Triads meet, there is the Center of the Worlds.
Let this sacred center be the boundary of all worlds, that my voice be carried and my vision see.
Now let the Fire open the Gate
Let the Well open the Gate
Let the Tree hold fast the Way Between.

Open as an eye of seeing
Open as a mouth of speaking

> *Open as an oaken door, between this Sacred Center and the Otherworlds.*
> *By the Keeper of Gates, and by my Will and Word, let the Gate be open!*

[13] Fill the horn or cup with ale and raise it, saying:

> *Gods and Dead and mighty Spirits, Powers of Land and Sky and Sea,*
> *By Fire and Well and sacred Tree, offerings I make to thee!*
>
> *To those who dwell below, to those who dwell above, to the tribes of spirits in land, sea or sky*
>
> *Hear your true worshipper (your name) as I make due sacrifice*
> *to the Dead, the Spirits & the Gods.*
>
> *O Mighty Ones, my Ancestors, my kindred; I your child honor you,*
> *and ask you draw near my hearth.*
> *You whose life and death creates my life, you whose wisdom upholds my wisdom,*
>
> *Elder Clans of the Wise, the Warriors and the Keepers of Land,*
> *Here I give you your due welcome.*
>
> *O Mighty Ancestors, I honor your presence, offering my love and worship.*
> *Be with me in my grove and in my heart, and accept this gift in token of my kinship.*

[14] Drink from the horn is spilled on the ground or into the bowl. Cry:

> *Ancestors, accept my sacrifice!*
>
> *O Noble Ones, my Allies, with whom I share the worlds, I ask you welcome me in your places.*
>
> *You who fill the land with wonder, Spirits of Stone and Stream, Red and Green*
>
> *Tribes of Spirits, the Peoples of the Otherworld,*
> *Here I give you your due welcome.*
>
> *O Noble Spirits, I honor your presence, offering my love and worship.*
>
> *Be with me in my grove and in my heart, and accept this gift in token of my friendship.*

[15] Drink from the horn is spilled on the ground or into the bowl. Cry:

> *Landspirits, accept my sacrifice!*
>
> *O Shining Ones, my Elders, Goddeses and Gods of All Realms,*
> *I ask you to draw near to my spirit.*
>
> *O Wisest and Mightiest, loving and comforting, wrathful and wild,*
> *you who sustain all the worlds,*
>
> *First Children of the Mother, the Tribe of the Goddess*
> *Here I give you your due welcome.*
>
> *O Shining Deities, I honor your presence, offering my love and worship.*
> *Be with me in my grove and in my heart, and accept this gift in token of my kinship.*

[16] Drink from the horn is spilled on the ground or into the bowl. Cry:

> *Shining Ones, accept my sacrifice!*

[17] Pause for a moment and feel and envision the Gods and Spirits approaching your Grove. Prepare a final offering, and gather up all your worship and aspiration toward the Gods and Spirits, as you make the final sacrifice, saying:

The Very Basics of Ritual

Mighty, Noble and Shining Ones, Turn your faces toward my Fire, and join me now in my Grove! Oh Host of the Holy, I call you on the Spirit Road; by the Three Realms and the Four Winds, by the World Tree's root and branch. By Fire's light and Well's might, come to my call, and accept my sacrifice! (make final offering)

[18] Take up your divining tool of choice and meditate on the patrons and on the intention of this rite. Cast for a simple omen, with this charm:

Spirit of the Gift, Spirit of the Song, Spirit of Destiny
Give me the gift of seeing, let me hear the song of the Turning of the Worlds
Mighty, Noble & Shining Ones, I have offered to you.
Now let the true sight be in me, the true speech be mine,
Answer me now, O spirits, what blessing do you offer me, in return for my offerings?

[19] Meditate on the omen, seek to understand what blessings the powers offer in return for the sacrifice. Then, compose of all this - the image, the intention, and the omen–into a single gestalt of energy.

With the omen in mind, call for the Blessing, saying:

As a Child of Earth, I call for the blessing of the Ancient Ones.
Holy Ones, give me the waters!

I open my heart to the blessing of the Powers.
Holy Ones, give me the waters!

And as I am blessed, let all the worlds be blessed.
Holy Ones, give me the waters.

[20] Refill the horn and breathe the combined energy current into the drink saying:

I pour the ale of inspiration, I draw water from the well of wisdom
I fill the cauldron of my spirit, with this drink.
I call upon (patron powers) to give to me as I have given to you, as a gift calls for a gift.
Oh Holy Powers, Gods and Dead and Spirits, hallow these waters! Let this vessel receive your power, spilled like the Mead of Inspiration, into my cup and into my spirit and soul and flesh.
I open my heart to the flow of your blessing, I, your child and worshipper.
Behold the waters of life!

[21] Reverently drink most of the blessing, perhaps sprinkling any object to be consecrated in the work as well. Meditate on the influx of spiritual current. Affirm the receiving of the Power, saying:

The worlds are in me, and I am in the worlds
The spirit in me is the spirit in the worlds

touch a bit of the drink to your belly, below the navel, saying:

Let this blessing be upon me and upon the world
my hair as the green forests, my flesh as the fertile soil, my bones as the ancient stones.

…touch a bit of the drink to your heart, saying:

Let this blessing be upon me and upon the world
my blood as the salt sea, my breath the rolling wind, my mind the cool shining moon.

…touch a bit of the drink to your forehead, saying:

> Let this blessing be upon me and upon the world
> my face as the shining sun, my thoughts as the grey clouds, my head crowned in stars
>
> Nine holy things in the world and in my self,
> That the Order of the World be True and Whole.
> By Gods, Dead and Spirits; By Fire, Well and Tree;
> The blessing flows and shines in me!
> So be it!

[22] If you have any remaining work, meditations, spells etc, they could be completed at this time. When all is done, give thanks, saying:

> By this work I am blessed, by the power of the Mighty, Noble and Shining Ones! Secure in their blessing, I go from the Grove into my life and work. I go with the blessing of the Gods in my head, and heart and loins. To all those who have aided me in this holy work, I give thanks.
>
> Triple Kindreds, Gods, Dead and Landspirits:
> I thank you for your presence in my small Grove.
> Shining Ones, Mighty Dead, Noble Spirits
> I thank you for your aid and blessing.

[23] Make a closing triskel over the Fire.

> Lord of the gates, lord of knowledge, I give you my thanks.
> Now let the Fire be flame, the Well be water,
> Let all be as it was before, save for the magic I have made
> Let the Gates be closed!

[24] Recenter and contemplate the entire working, and end, saying:

> To the Mother I give thanks, for ever upholding my life and my work.
>
> The fire, the well the sacred tree
> Flow and flame and grow in me!
> Peace and blessings to all beings,
> The rite is ended!

Hearth Cultures & High Days

To give readers an idea of how ADF's eight festivals might be celebrated according to the variety of Indo-European hearth cultures, we present you with the following eight summaries. It is important to keep in mind that these summaries are jumping-off points, and readers are encouraged to build their own traditions celebrating the Gods and seasons.

THE BRITISH ('WELSH') GODS AND SPIRITS
Deities of the Grove

- **Earth Mother**: Dôn, mother of the gods

- **Gatekeepers**: Manawydan, Arawn, and Gwyn ap Nudd (Arawn and Gwyn are sometimes identified as the same figure)

- **Bardic Deity**: Ceridwen, keeper of the Cauldron of Inspiration.

- **Outdwellers**: there are various malevolent forces, such as the Coraniaid, the evil dwarves who wreaked havoc by hearing everything and distorting the message before it was recieved. In ritual, it is best to keep forces like the Coraniaid at bay. The Tylwyth Teg, while also classified as Spirits, can be malevolent as well, and should be kept in mind.

Three Kindreds

- **The Gods**: The gods are in two groups: the Children of Dôn, the Shining gods of skill and rule–such as the three brothers Gwydion (the wizard/bard), Gofannon (the smith), and Amaethon (the farmer), and their father Beli Mawr, king from whom some of the great houses of Wales claim decent; and the Children of Llyr, who are more tied to land and underworld (especially Brân the Blessed, possessor of the Cauldron of Rebirth and leader of the Otherworld Feast).

- **The Spirits**: not only the Tylwyth Teg–the Fair Folk, i.e. fairies—but all the spirits that inhabit the natural world. Some might include the Red Dragon of Wales itself, embodiment of the land.

- **The Ancestors**: the noble dead who've gone before us–legendary heroes like enigmatic King Arthur, bards like Taliesin and Aneirin, lawgivers like Hywel Dda, later figures like the poet Dafydd ap Gwillim and freedom-fighter Owain Glyndwr, as well as our own ancestors.

The High Days:

Lore for the High Days is largely drawn from the "Four Branches of the Mabinogi" and "Culhwch and Olwen", as well as Welsh folk customs:

- **Calan Gaeaf (Beginning of Winter)** - November 1, and first of the three Ysprydnos or "Spirit Nights"
  Lore: The year–and the "Mabinogi"–begins with Pwyll's encounter with Arawn, king of Annwfn, who in order to pay a debt has Pwyll fight his enemy Hafgan–"summer-white". Pwyll visits the Otherworld (a common theme for this time of year), and with it gives rise to the winter half of the year. The trip to Annwfn coincides with the old practices of the "dumb supper" for the dead and divination.

- Alban Gaeaf/Canol Gaeaf (Winter Solstice/Midwinter) - December 21ish
  Lore: This is the time when, in "Culhwch and Olwen", Mabon, the lost Great Son, is found again by Arthur and his knights, thus paving the way for victory over the monstrous boar Twrch Trwyth; in the "Mabinogi", it can be seen as the time of Lleu's death, transformation, and recovery–much like the sun. Finally, this is around the time of the Feast of Epona, the Gaulish horse goddess, which coincides with the Welsh tradition of the Mari Llwyd, a hobbyhorse procession from this holiday, which hearkens back to Rhiannon, the Welsh Great Queen and horse goddess.

- Calan Gwanwyn (First day of Spring) - February 1
  Lore: The Mabinogi tale of Branwen is recalled–like Brigit she can also be seen as a hearth Goddess, since much of her story, like this holiday, is connected with fire. Also, the tale of the Cauldron of Rebirth fits the beginning of spring.

- Alban Eilir (Spring Equinox) - March 21ish
  Lore: Pwyll's courtship of Rhiannon, and the subsequent birth of Pryderi, who is stolen and not found again until Calan Haf.

- Calan Haf (The beginning of Summer) - May 1, and second of the three Ysprydnos or "Spirit Nights".
  Lore: This day has a wealth of lore attached to it: from being one of the dates for the riding of the Wild Hunt, to the yearly battle of Gwyn ap Nudd and Gwythr over the hand of Creidddylad, to the finding of the stolen child Pryderi in a stable.

- Alban Hefin (Summer Solstice) - June 21ish, and third of the three Ysprydnos or "Spirit Nights".
  Lore: this is one of the nights when the Tylwyth Teg are most active. From the Mabinogi, Otheworld Feast of the Assembly of the Noble Head, lead by Brân the Blessed, is recalled.

- Calan Elfed (Beginning of Autumn) - August 1
  Lore: the story of Lleu Llaw Gyffes from the fourth branch of the "Mabinogi".

- Gwyl Cynhaeaf (Feast of Harvest) - September 21ish
  Lore: The Mabinogi story of Manawydan and the plague of mice takes place at harvest time; his savvy not only saves the harvest, but his family.

THE GAELIC GODS AND SPIRITS
The Gods of the Grove

- **Earth Mother**: Danu, the Eldest Mother; Aine, Queen in the Mound; any River Goddess, such as Boann

- **Gatekeeper**: Manannan is often asked to keep the Gate, though some work with Ogma.

- **Outdwellers**: The Giants–most commonly called fomhoire among the Gaels, the giants, or men of the sea, were the primal opponents of the Gods in the Book of Invasions tales.

Concepts of the Kindreds

- **The Spirits**: are a complex issue in Gaelic lore – Some seem like the bright courts of noble humans, others like predators in the bushes of the Otherworld. Sometimes they are called collectively, the Aos Sidhe, or Daoine Sidhe – the People of the Mound.

- **The Dead**: In Irish tales the Dead are said to go to the island called Teach Duinne, off the Munster coast. There they are hosted by Donn, the Lord of the Dead, and perhaps sail away westward in time. Classical authors say the Druids taught reincarnation, though that is not plain in all the tales.

- **The Gods**: are the First Family of the local tales. In much of Gaelic lore they are the Children of a primal parent figure called Danu or Don, a figure lost in the past. Her children become the Kings and Queens of the Gods, and are joined by other local Mighty Ones, deified humans and powerful Outsiders.

The High Days

- **The November Feast**: Samhain (Summer's End): The Feast of the Dead. Dagda & Morrigan mate in the River. Donn gathers the Host of the Dead. The Sidhe burn Tara. The Old Woman (Calleach) reigns. The cattle are slain for winter, and the harvest is fully in the barns.

- **The February Feast**: Imbolc (In the Belly): The Feast of the Hearth. The Feast of Brigid, who is Hearth Mother and Triple Power of Inspiration. Milk returns to the ewes, bringing fresh food after winter. The Brigid Dolly and Girdle bring Her blessings.

- **The May Feast**: Bealtainne (Bright Fire): The Feast of the Landspirits. The Earth-mother regains her youth and the Young King, Mac Oc, reigns. The tribes of the sidhe-folk arrive in the world. The Fire of purification and blessing seeks the luck of summer, growth and gain.

- **The August Feast**: Lughnassadh (Feast of Lugh): The Feast of the Warrior. The Feast of Lugh, the Victorious Child. The enemies of the harvest are driven away by the power of the sky. Pilgrimages and the peace-fair, and especially the warrior games in honor of Lugh's foster-mother an Earth Goddess.

The Quarter Days are not very clearly observed in Gaelic lore. Some Gaelic countries have absorbed lore from Viking or Norman incomers that has become as 'Irish' as the shamrock, but many Gaelic Groves and solitaries use the solstices and equinoxes for more general honoring of the land and the season, perhaps thus:

- **Winter Solstice**: Hearth, Kin and a Groaning Table-full. Gathering in fellowship and a spirit of accord, over the bounty of the year's harvest. Ancestors remain important in this Samhain season.

- **Spring Equinox**: Blessing the Seed and the Furrow. Preparation of land and life for new growth, seed-blessing charms and customs. Lots of fertility work, to bring the year's wealth.

- **Summer Solstice**: Fire and Frolic among the Flowers. Work and play as the crop is tended and the warriors are abroad in their work. The Landwights continue to be important in the season following Bealtaine.

- **Fall Equinox**: The Reaping and the Gathering In: Gaining the good of the year's work, evaluating and profit-taking, with customs to honor the Grain and the Reaper.

Gaulish Gods, Spirits and Festivals
Dēvī Nemetoni - The Gods of the Grove

- **The Earth Mother**: Dānū, the primal goddess, associated with Europe's principal river, the Danube. Local river goddesses; where no Celtic name is retreviable, she could simply be addressed as Dēvā, Goddess. In addition, there is the personification of Gaul herself, Litāvī.

- **The Gatekeeper**: Cernunnos, the liminal psychopomp god, who represents the connection between the lands of the tribe and the wild.

- **The Hearth Goddess**: Brigantī, also known as Brigindū. In Irish lore she is better known as Brigid, goddess of poetry and craft, but her earliest patronage is the domestic hearth.

- **The Outsiders**: Ancenetlī. Not gods, but significant- these represent forces and powers which have no relationship with the Tribe, sometimes hostile but mainly just indifferent.

Trīcenetlos - The Three Kindreds

- **The Gods**: Dēvī. The first children of the goddess Dānū. The shining ones, the undying, the givers of goods.

- **The Ancestors**: Senistres. The spirits of the blessed dead. While for most of the year they dwell in Andumnos, the otherworld, they can still be called upon to render assistance to their descendants.

- **The Spirits**: There are many other miscellaneous spirits, including spirits of a location (genii loci in Latin, brogidēvī in Gaulish) and other natural features. Most familiar to humans, however, are the Cucullātī, represented as small, hooded figures with prominent phalluses: these are the spirits of the household, to be propriated with milk or ale.

Ivostoves - The High Days

- **November Feast**: Samonis, the beginning of the winter half of the year. A feast celebrating the end of the year and the cycle of death and rebirth. On this day the ancestors are released from Amdumnos to feast with the living. A feast dedicated to Sucellos and Nantosuelta, deities of the Otherworld.

- **February Feast**: Usmolgos, also known as Ambivolcos. A feast celebrating Brigantī's rekindling of the world's hearth-fire, the promise of spring, the return of the light and the purification of the home. An appropriate time to do the spring cleaning!

- **May Feast**: Belotenes, the feast of the shining fire. Marking the beginning of the summer half of the year, it is at this feast that the flocks and those who tend them would be purified before being taken to their summer pastures. A time to celebrate fertility and reproduction.

- **August Feast**: Oinacos Lugous, the Gatherings of Lugus. The harvest begins, the late summer thunderstorms arrive and the Tribe gathers together, to buy, sell and show off. A feast of martial and physical prowess.

With regard to the quarter days, the calendar of Coligny does not seem to mark the equinoxes, although the summer and winter solstices are clearly marked.

- **Winter Solstice**: Dēvoriuros, the feast of midwinter plenty. The harvest is in, the livestock have been slaughtered and it's time to snuggle in and celebrate the bounty of the gods and the promise of renewal against the darkness. Dedicated to the goddess Matronā and her son Maponos, born on this day.

- **Vernal Equinox**: Dius Aratri, the Day of the Plough, a day under the tutelage of of Ambaxtonos, god of farmers, and Taranis, god of thunder. Agricultural tools are blessed on this day, and in Northern Europe the equinoctal gales are very much present!

- **Summer Solstice**: Mediosamos, the midpoint of summer. A day of wildfire- not the safe hearth fire but the dangerous wildfire. Celebrated by an all-night vigil by a hilltop bonfire throughout Europe.

- **Autumnal Equinox**: Diocomrextios, the day for settling all disputes. Contracts would be renewed on this day. A day to celebrate community and the maintenance of good relationships which bind it together.

THE HELLENIC GODS AND SPIRITS
The Gods of the Grove

- **Earth Mother**: Gaea (Gaia, Ge), Mother of All, primeval earth goddess, whose consort is Ouranos; Rhea, Great Mother, Mother of the Gods, Mother of All, queen of heaven, whose consort is Kronos; any local river or mountain spirit.

- **Gatekeeper**: Hermes, the Guide, Messenger of the Gods, Interpreter; Hekate, of the Crossroads, of the Three-Ways, Guardian, Key-holder; Iris, Messenger, goddess of the rainbow.

- **Outdwellers**: The Titans, who were overthrown by the Olympians, although some, such as Hekate, sided with Zeus and the Olympians; the Gigantes, who battled the Olympians and were defeated; the Keres, spirits of violent or untimely death; often Eris, goddess of strife, discord, contention, and rivalry.

Concepts of the Kindreds

- **The Spirits**: Daemones, including nymphs of rivers, mountains, trees, clouds, and seas, spirits of the wild such as satyrs, silenoi, and panes.

- **The Dead**: Ancestors were honored at their graves. The Heroes, who were communal ancestors often holding powers of healing and aid in battle, also received cult. Some in the Greek world, such as the initiates of Eleusis, looked forward to a blessed afterlife. Others, such as the Orphics, followed a path of reincarnation.

- **The Gods**: Primarily the Olympians but including many other beings as well. A few mortals, such as Herakles and Asklepios, even managed to become immortal gods. The gods take interest in mortal affairs, responding to pleas and occasionally walking the earth in various guises. They are often associated with the heights of Olympos, but many are at home on the earth and in the underworld as well.

The High Days

The Mediterranean climate differs from that of Northern Europe, with the barren time in the heat of summer and the fertile time in fall, winter, and spring. Festivals were often civic, not necessarily connected to cycles of crop, herd, or sun. Each city and town often had its own calendar and cycle of feasts, and when a new colony was founded, the old festivals were not carried over but new ones were established. The festivals below are but a selection, mainly from the most complete calendar that comes down to us, that of Athens. Solar phenomena are listed as they would appear in Greece (i.e. northern hemisphere).

- **August Feast - The Panathenaia**: feast of Athene, goddess of the city. A new peplos, or robe, is presented to Athena for her cult statue. A procession and various competitions are held.

- **Autumn Equinox - The Eleusinian Mysteries**: feast of Demeter and Kore. New initiates are brought into the mysteries of life and death.

- **November Feast - The Thesmophoria**: feast of Demeter, a women's festival. This is the time of the autumn sowing. The remains of sacrificial offerings, thrown into pits earlier (probably at Skira) are brought up, mixed with seed corn, and placed on altars.

- **Winter Solstice - The Oreibasia**: feast of Dionysos, a festival of the wild women (maenads) held at Delphi. Delegations of maenads from many cities gather to dance in ecstasy.

- **February Feast - The Anthesteria**: feast of Dionysos, Ariadne, and Cthonic Hermes. New jars of wine are opened, the young are initiated into the community in a rite of silent drinking, Dionysos and Ariadne celebrate a sacred marriage, and the ancestors receive a pottage of honeyed grains.

- **Spring Equinox - The City or Greater Dionysia**: feast of Dionysos. Phalloi are carried in procession, and competitions in theater, poetry, and the arts are held.

- **May Feast - Thargelia**: Feast of Apollon and Artemis, birthday of the twins. The city and fields are purified by driving out a scapegoat. The eiresione, or May bough, is carried to the temple of Apollon or to the doors of private houses. The first fruits of the harvest are dedicated to Apollon and Artemis, and celebrations are held with music and dance.

- **Summer Solstice - Skira**: feast of Demeter, Kore, Athena, and Poseidon. This is the time of grain threshing. Many believe this is the season when Kore descends to the realm of Hades. Offerings are thrown into subterranean pits (if not in this festival, then around this time), to be retrieved in the Thesmophoria. The New Year follows.

An alternative Winter Solstice entry:. Winter Solstice - The Rural Dionysia: feast of Dionysos. A procession is held, carrying phalloi and other things. Celebrants hop on wineskins. Some believe comedy evolved from this festival.

The Norse Gods and Spirits
The Gods of the Grove

- **Earth Mother**: The goddesses Nerthus or Jord are the common choices; our knowledge of Nerthus is much earlier (from Tacitus) than that of Jord.

- **Gatekeeper**: The god Heimdall, as the guardian of Bifrost, is frequently chosen. Other choices in an ADF context include Freya (as a psychopomp, for choosing among the dead, and for her wanderings after Odr), and Odin (also for his wanderings and from the psychopompic aspects of being a god of death and hanging on Yggdrasil, the world tree). Some Norse ADF rites approach the Gatekeeper from a warding or guarding aspect, calling on Thor or Syn (a handmaiden of Frigg). This is an abridged list; there are many additional possible gatekeeper choices among the pantheon.

* **Bardic Patrons**: The god Bragi, with his focus on the skaldic (bardic) arts, is oft selected. Others include Odin, for his role in poetic inspiration; Kvasir, in his role as the first poet, from whose blood was brewed the Mead of Inspiration; and Saga, handmaiden of Frigg and mistress of tale-telling.

Concepts of the Kindreds

* **The Shining Ones**: The Shining Ones, or Gods and Goddesses, are divided into the tribes of the Aesir and Vanir. Generally, the Aesir powers and the Vanir who live with them in Asgard (Nerthus, Njord, Frey, and Freya) are honored. They are generally honored with offerings of alcohol, especially mead, though food, often bread, also plays a frequent role.

* **The Nature Spirits**: The various tribes and families of land, nature, and house spirits are often referred to collectively as the Landvaettir. Included in that broad term are the Hidden folk of the land (HuldrFolk) such as trolls, wights, elves, & mosswives; plant and animal spirits; as well as the various entities commonly found in/around the home. Offerings to these beings are regularly made throughout the year, whether a bowl of milk on the hearth, or a small loaf for the Mosswives (not caraway!) in the garden at the beginning of Spring

* **The Ancestors**: The Disir and Alfar are frequently considered to be ancestral spirits. The Disir are female ancestor-spirits who watch over families; the Alfar are often considered to be male ancestor-spirits who watch over land, businesses and/or prosperity. Offerings to ancestors took place at burial mounds, and descendants would sometimes sit out on an ancestor's burial mound to get advice.

The High Days

* **Winter Solstice**: Yule was perhaps the most important holiday of the year. The celebration began with Mother's Night on the eve of the solstice, which was focused on honoring the goddesses. The celebration would continue for twelve days with a burning Yule log, feasting, and oath-taking (though oaths were important year-round in a Norse context). Often a boar, sacred to Frey, was roasted during Yule. There are many appropriate deities to honor at this time; an abridged list would include Thor, for warding the folk; Odin, as leader of the Wild Hunt; Frey, for strength through the winter and fertility in the year to come; Baldur, who some consider as returning from the dead on the solstice; and Skadhi, for her association with winter activities.

* **February Cross-quarter**: Charming of the Plough, a time of preparing for Spring and the planting season, blessing the tools of the planting and honoring the fields. The Lore of Frey and Gerd is often retold. Loaves, cakes, or even a leek are often placed in the ground as offerings to Nerthus, or sometimes Thor.

* **Vernal Equinox**: It has been deduced that the Anglo-Saxons honored Eostre, Goddess of Spring and fertility, at this time; in a Norse context, Idunna (eye-DUNE-ah) would be an appropriate choice.

- **May Cross-quarter**: Walpurgisnacht, May Day in the modern day. The themes of this holiday revolve around magic (for the eve) and love (for the day), making this close to modern Pagans' sense of Beltane.

- **Summer Solstice**: Midsummer, which is among the larger of Norse High Days. Bonfires were, and still are, a frequent focus of the celebration. This is a time for celebrating the community and fire/sun gods.

- **August Cross-quarter**: Freyfaxi (Frey's-Mane) or Loaf-fest; start of the grain harvest and the first loaf of bread, historically marked by horse-racing, horse-fighting, and other equestrian activities; this was when the Thing was held in Iceland, so honoring Tyr would be also appropriate. Some would also link this start of the wheat harvest to the cutting of Sif's hair.

- **Autumnal Equinox**: often Thor and Sif are honored for their linkage to agriculture and the harvest; alternately, see Winternights below.

- **November Cross-quarter**: The Full Moon after the Equinox is Winternights, focused on honoring the Ancestors (especially the Disir), the coming of winter, and giving thanks for the stored abundance.

THE VEDIC GODS AND SPIRITS
The Gods of the Grove

- **Earth Mother**: Prthivi, the Earth; Dyavaprhivi, the duality of "Heaven and Earth"; Sarasvati, "abounding in water"

- **Gatekeeper**: Agni, "fire," without whom sacrifice cannot be made, for it is he who conveys the sacrifice to the gods and brings the gods to sit upon the sacrificial grasses.

- **Outdwellers**: the Asuras, Panis, and Dasa - the demons of the celestial realm, the upper air, and the atmosphere (respectively), associated with darkness and the stealing and hording of wealth and cattle. Also, Vrtra, "the encompasser," who has stolen the waters.

Concepts of the Kindreds

- **The Spirits**: The Vedas spend little time on the spirits of nature (and generally divides them into "helpful" and "injurious," like the cow and the snake respectively), but the natural world is vitally important and often praised. Generally, just as humans exist in a natural world where various animals are important, so too have the Gods, and there are many deified animals and plants. Large trees are known as vanaspati ("lord of the forest"), and the forest as a whole is invoked as divine under the name Aranyani, the jungle goddess.

- **The Dead**: The Ancestors exist in the highest heavens, where the king of the dead, Yama, the first man, revels with the deities. Heroes and those who bestow the most liberal sacrifices are counted as chief among the dead. The Pitrs ("fathers") are the first ancestors, and they are said to come with the gods to the sacrifice.

- **The Gods**: Closer to physical phenomenon than the gods of other pantheons, the Vedic gods are immanent and ever present. Fire (Agni), sun (Surya), and dawn (Usas) are all deities whose form is seen when kindled, in the sky, or at dawn, respectively.

The Very Basics of Ritual

They did not begin as immortal, but won immortality; represent the chief powers of nature; and follow the rta, or Cosmic Order. They are often divided into three groups: Terrestrial, Atmospheric, and Celestial, representing the three divisions of the cosmos.

The High Days

The feast days of the ADF calendar do not match well with Vedic religion, but eight festivals around those times are not difficult to work with. Here, half the year is devoted to Indra's victories, and the other half devoted to other gods and spirits:

- **The Early Winter Feast**: Yama's Feast. Yama was the first man to die and the first to find his way through death. Celebrating King Yama and the ancestors who have joined him is very appropriate.

- **The Mid-Winter Feast**: The Freeing of the Sun. The demon Svarbhanu is said to have stolen the sun and replaced it with darkness. Indra fights the demon, and Atri replaces the sun in the heavens.

- **The Late Winter Feast**: Valamurja, "Breaking the demon Vala". Vala steals the cows and places them in a dark cave, which Indra pierces (along with Agni, Soma, Brhaspati, and others) the door of to allow the cows to return. In this story, ghee is found in the cows; ghee is often poured to Agni in sacrifice, and so this is also a story of obtaining the sacrifice for use.

- **The Spring Feast**: The Production of Dawn. At one time, Usas is said to refuse to appear, which means that the sun cannot continue in his course. Again, Indra is the hero, breaking open her wain and releasing the cows to begin the day.

- **The Early Summer Feast**: Vrtraturya, "Conquest of Vrtra." A celebration of Indras's defeat of Vrtra and the releasing of the waters is well-timed when the thunderstorms of late spring and early summer are rolling through.

- **The Mid-Summer Feast**: Agnihotr. Agni must be sustained, and as such, the Agnihotr would be a good feast at the middle of the summer, giving fuel to the sun and providing vitality to help the sun through the year at this time, when it expends the most effort.

- **The Late Summer Feast**: Tvastr's Feast. Tvastr is a skilled workman who creates many of the tools of the gods, including Indra's thunderbolt. Displays of skill and ability would be good for this feast, as would warrior games.

- **The Autumn Feast**: Soma Feast. Soma is a drink much praised in the Vedas for its intoxicating (and possibly hallucinogenic) nature. While the soma plant itself is lost to history, the concept of an inspirative drink that is made by "pressing" is not. A ritual around the winning of the Soma or the inspiration the drink brings would not be out of place.

A Reconstructed Proto-Indo-European Pantheon
The Gods of the Grove

- **Earth Mother**: Dhéghōm Mātr "Earth Mother"

- **Gatekeeper**: Xáusōs "Rising" Goddess of the Dawn, where the gods enter the world. Or, especially in rituals already directed towards Xáusōs, you might use Xákwōm Népōt "Close Relative of the Waters," who is a god of a well whose fiery water introduces power to the Cosmos.

- **God of Grove Unity**: Xáryomen "Lord of the People"
- **The Outdwellers**: Hógwhēs "The Snakes," the chief of which is slain by the Striking God (Perkwūnos) as part of the creation of the Cosmos.

Concepts of the Kindreds

- **The Xánsūs (sing. Xánsus)**: "The Spirits." Numinous beings connected with trees, stones, rivers, and other elements of nature are found throughout the entire Indo-European world, and can be assumed for the Proto-Indo-Europeans. They are not necessarily our friends, but it's best to be on their good side.
- **The Dead**: W'kpotēs "Lords of the Household" The dead live in the land of Yemos, but may be called to rituals, especially in the spring. They include not only the genetic ancestors, but cultural ones. They are sometimes closely connected with places.
- **The Gods**: Déiwōs (sing. Déiwos) "The Shining Ones." As their name implies, they are connected with light, as well as with the natural order of the Cosmos. They are sometimes called "Givers of Gifts" and "Immortal Ones."

The High Days

Spring was a very busy time for the Proto-Indo-Europeans. It began with the Spring Equinox, which was the New Year (the beginning of the year, not the end). Associated with Xáusōs and Diwós Sunú ("Sons of the God"). The return of Light.

- **Planting**: At the time appropriate for the area. Dedicated to Perkwūnos "Striker" or "Oak God," who brings the rains and fertilizes the earth.
- **Recreation of the Cosmos**: This could be done at the same time as the equinox, or soon afterwards. It involves a ritual repetition of the sacrifice by which the Cosmos was originally organized.
- **May Feast**: Sending out of the Herds. A feast of purification after winter. In PIE days this was the time when the herds and the youth would go out to the pastures, both being purified by fire and smoke first.
- **Midsummers**: Probably not celebrated by the PIEs. Today it might be celebrated in honor of the sun goddess, Sawélyosyo Dhugtēr, and/or Xákwōm Népōt, god of fire in water.
- **Fall Equinox**: Two possible festivals: Bringing in the herds. This time the herds are brought back from the pastures, and must be reincorporated into society or Harvest: Dedicated to Dhéghōm Mātr. One can be celebrated at the equinox, and the other at the end of October.
- **October Feast**: Sometime between Yule and the Spring Equinox, especially right before the equinox, was likely another feast of the dead, again with feasting with them, but with an emphasis on purification from the old, dead year.
- **Winter Solstice**: The end of the year, and the feast of the dead. The W'kpotēs are called to return, feasted, and then dismissed.

The Very Basics of Ritual

THE ROMAN PANTHEON
The Gods of the Grove

* **Earth Mother:** Tellus Terra Mater (Tellus, Mother Earth, the personification of the productive powers of Earth); Ceres (goddess of growth, renewal and grain)

* **Gatekeeper:** Janus Patulcius, Opener of Doors/Janus Clusivius, Closer of Doors; Mercury, God of travelers and messenger of the Gods

* **Outdwellers:** Gods of chaos, disharmony and anarchy; the elder gods (the Titans, although this is more Greek); gods of the wilds (with caveats for seasonal appropriateness)

Concepts of the Kindred

* **The Spirits:** The Penates, spirits of the pantry and cupboards, protect household supplies and ensure that it does not go hungry or is unable to offer hospitality. The Lares (plural of Lar) are spirits of the land - both domestic and wild. Those who live with the household are the Lar Familiaris, the spirits of the home. Outside there are two types of land: claimed and unclaimed. Lares may be domestic, urban, and wild. Boundary spirits and deities maintain the balance between inside and the outside; city and country; tame and wild; chaos and order. Among these are Janus, the god of doors and Terminus, god of boundaries. Beyond the Terminii are the wild and unpredictable gods of the forest, Silvanus and Faunus, whose realms include all the uncultivated land beyond the boundaries of the owned and settled land.

* **The Dead:** Romans didn't speculate much about the fate of the dead, but paid them enormous respect - either out of simple regard or outright fear. Feasts of the dead are clustered in February and May. Funeral rituals in Rome were quite elaborate, and families would keep wax renditions of their ancestors' faces in their homes, which they would process through the streets for each family funeral. Some historical figures, such as Numa and several of the Caesars, came to be thought of as deities, in a sort of metamorphosis from Ancestor to Deity.

* **The Gods:** Deities acknowledged and honored in Rome include the Fathers of Rome, Romulus & Remus; King Numa; the Archaic Triad (Jupiter, Mars and Quirinus) and the Capitoline Trio (Jupiter, Juno and Minerva); numerous mystery cults & foreign gods (Cybele, Isis, Mithras, etc.) Flamens (priests) were appointed to serve specific deities: Carmentis, Ceres, Falacer, Flora, Furrina, Jupiter, Mars, Palatua, Pomona, Portunes, Quirinus, Vulcan, and Volturnus. Other major deities include Apollo, Diana, Juno, Mercury, Minerva, Neptune, Venus, Divus Augustus, Divus Julius, Fortuna, Pluto, Sol, and Vesta.

The High Days

The climate and culture of southern Europe are quite different from the northern climates that produced our eight-fold year. Roman neopagans have made many choices about reconciling those calendars. Rather than present an artificial construct we simply present this summary of the Roman holy days.

* **March:** the season of reawakening and renewal, the first month of the year and the beginning of campaigning season. Major events include: Equirria, Mamuralia (14); Anna Perenna and Jovi (15); Liberalia, Libera, Agonalia (17); Quinquartus (19); Tubilustrium (23); Luna (31).

* **April**: a very busy month in the Roman calendar; most holidays are associated with earth deities. Major feasts include: Veneralia (1); Megalesian Games (4-10); Games of Ceres (12-19); Iovi Vitori, Iovi Literatit (13); Fordicidia (15); Parilia (21); Vinalia Priori (23); Robigalia (25); Floralia (April 27-May 3).

* **May**: the key celebrations are of a somber nature, mainly associated with the dead and underworld; major festivals include: Bona Dea (1); Lemuria (9, 11, 13); Mercurius (15); Agonalia (21); Tubilustrium (23); Fortuna (25); Feria Conceptivae (Ambarvalia) (25).

* **June**: The first part of June was considered an unlucky time; the Vestalia, the first major festival in June, was when the refuse from the temple of Vesta was cleaned out and dumped into the Tiber. Major festivals include: Juno Moneta (1); Bellona (3); Hercules (4); Vestalia (9); Matralia, (11); Feriae Jovi (Quinquartus minusculae) (13); Summanus (20); Fortunae (24); Ludi Taurei quinquennales (25, 26); Hercules Musagetes (30).

* **July**: the hottest and driest month of the year, is the considered to be Jupiter's month. Its primary concerns include keeping crops watered and the ever-present fear of uncontrolled fires. Also during July the virtues of the Roman matrons and the class of knights (Equites) were celebrated. Major festivals include: Juno and Felicitati (1); Poplifugia (5); Games Of Apollo (6-13); Fortuna Muliebris; Pales; (6); Nones of the Wild Fig; Consus (7); Vitula (8); Honor & Virtue (17); Lucaria (19, 21); Concordia (22); Neptunalia (23); Furrinalia (25); Fortune of the Day (30).

* **August**: by August, the harvest would be nearly complete on most of the Italian peninsula. The month was protected by Ceres, and sacrifices were also made to Spes, Salus & Diana. Events include: Spes; Victory (1); Festival of Salus (5); Sol Indigites (9); Festival of Hercules; Venus Victrix (12); Festival of Diana; Festival of Vortumnus; Fortuna Equestri; Hercules Invictus; Caster & Pollux; Flora (13); Portunalia; Janus (17); Vinalia Rustica (19); Consualia (21); Volcanalia (23); Festival of Luna (24); Opiconsivia (25); Volturnalia (27); Sun and Moon (28).

* **September**: a month of relaxation; there were lots of games, but not many festivals. The campaigning season would be over, and September marks the lull between the harvest and the vintage. The month is protected by Vulcan. Events include: Jupiter & Juno (1); Ludi Romani (4-19); Jupiter Stator (5); 'Banquet' with Jupiter (and later Juno, Minerva) (13); Apollo (23); Venus Genetrix (26).

* **October**: marks the end of the campaign season, and so there are related festivals in honor of Mars, the October Horse, and the purification of the army so that soldiers could then be fit inhabitants of the city again. The Mediterranean agricultural season closes in October for the most important of crop in Rome: grapes. Major events include: Juno Sororio, Janus Curiatius (1); Fast of Ceres (4); Mundus is opened (5); Jove Fulgar, Juno Quiriti (7); Juno Moneta (10); Meditrinalia (11); Fontanalia (13); Feast of Jupiter, October Horse, Capitoline Games (15); Armilustrium (19).

* **November**: Since the Italian peninsula has a relatively mild climate, there is a still lots of field work to be done in November; however, most of the month was absorbed with the Plebian Games (Ludi Plebii) (4-17). Other major events include: Mundus is opened (8); Feria Iovi, Feronia, Fortunae Primigeniae (13).

The Very Basics of Ritual

- **December**: the beginning of winter, is under Vesta's protection. Major events include: Bona Dea (3); Faunalia (5); Tiber (8); Agonolia; Septimontium (11); Consualia (15); Saturnalia (17-23); Opalia. (19); Divine Angerona; Hercules, Ceres (21); Larentalia (23).

- **January**: sacred to Janus and is a slack month, added to the calendar by Julius Caesar. Major events include: Aesculapio, Vediovis (1); Feriae Concpetivae (moveable) Compitalia (3-5); Agonalia (9); Carmentalia (11, 15); Iuturnae (11); Feria Conceptivae (27); Sementivae or Paganalia (a moveable feast around the 27th).

- **February**: February's name indicates its relation to death and purification. It is the last month of the year and marks the official beginning of Spring (February 5). Major events include: Juno Sospita, Queen Mother (1); Concordia (5); Faunus (13); Fornicalia (13-17); Parentalia (13-21 or 24); Lupercalia (15); Quirinalia (17); Feralia (21); Caristia (22); Terminalia (23); Regifugium (24).

Summary

What is Ritual?

Ritual is a repeated pattern of things done, things said, and things thought.

Spiritual ritual uses those things to link ordinary human awareness with the realms of the Gods and Spirits.

Basics of Ritual

It is easy to begin working ritual, but skill develops with experience.

- Every ritual must have a clear intention.
- Rituals are built on patterns of myth and symbol - ancient, reconstructed and modern.
- Druidic ritual is timed by the cycles of Sun, Moon and Earth.
- Ritual uses symbolic objects as 'tools' of the ritual trade.

The Primary Tools of ADF ritual

- Water cauldron (Well)
- Fire container (Fire)
- Altar pillar, tree or stone (Tree)

Secondary Tools

- Offering Bowl
- Vessel of Blessing
- Robe or Lamen (symbolic pendant, ring or torc)
- Various offerings and special symbols as required by the rite.
- Techniques of focusing awareness, ('altered states of awareness') calm the body and mind and open the self to the symbols of the rite.

Working Ritual

1. **Preparation**: Prepare the location; count your offerings and Tools; be familiar with the ritual; be calm, clean and focused.
2. **Set-up**: Create the center with the Fire, Well & Tree, set any special symbols nicely around them. Have any offerings, scripts, etc., ready to hand. Finally, count your offerings.
3. **Mind**: When you are ready to begin, and have taken your place at the Hallows, find your stillness and your power. Be sure to pause occasionally during the rite to renew your basic trance and connection with Earth and Sky.
4. **Work**: As you work your way through the words, actions and visualizations of the ritual, keep your body balanced and relaxed, your motions controlled and your voice clear and sure.
5. **Ending**: Never begin a ritual without ending it. Work the closing rites calmly and with a sense of gratitude and wonder.

Finally, the best way to begin to practice ritual is simply to begin. Choose one of the simple rituals we provide here. Set up a Shrine if you like, as we instruct in the second part of this guide, or just gather a set of tools to be set up at need. Find the first rounds of tools wherever you can—you probably have what you need at home. You can always find Just The Right Thing later. Practice the very basic entrancements as you begin, and work your way through a rite. Open your mind to the ideas and images of the rite, and be ready to approach, even by a little, the Gods and Spirits.

Part 7

A Working Full Druidic Ritual

The Outline of ADF Druidic Ritual

1. **Preparation**: All participants make certain they know their intention, and have a clear understanding of the order of the coming rite. A preliminary entrancement prepares the mind.

2. **Procession**: The participants go from ordinary space into ritual space.

3. **Opening Prayers**: The rite begins with a clear statement of beginning. The most traditional ADF opening prayers include a greeting and general request of the Gods and Spirits to bless the rite, then a special offering is made to the Earth Mother. Other preliminary offerings are often added.

4. **Statement of Purpose**: The intention of the rite is clearly stated, along with the Gods of the Occasion, and other material intended to focus and direct the minds of the participants.

5. **The Sacred Center**: The earliest forms of the rite used only the Fire as symbol of the center - other symbols have been added by various waves of our liturgists. Our most common current pattern uses Fire, Well & Tree, each of these being honored, or hallowed in this section of the rite.

6. **Completing the Cosmology**: Other aspects of the cultural cosmology of the rite are established or invoked, depending on the ethnicity and tastes of the participants. Land, Sea & Sky; Underworld, Midrealm, Heavens; Wise Ones, Warriors, Farmers; etc.

7. **Opening the Gate**: In the fully established center, an offering is made to the God who keeps Gates, in whatever ethnic system is being used, and the image of a Gate opening is used to bring our Sacred Center nearer to the world of the Gods and Spirits.

8. **General Offerings To and Invocations of The Spirits**: These invocations bring together the sacred beings of whatever ethnic system is being worked. It is common in our work to describe these as the Gods, the Dead & the Spirits, but this simple set of categories can always be made more specific for specific cultures.

9. **Honoring the Deities of The Rite**: The specific deities under whom the rite is being worked are invoked and offered to. This may include any specific customs or traditions associated with the deities, or with the seasonal or magical intention of the rite. In some cases, the rite may be worked to all the Kindreds in general, in which case this step may be omitted.

10. **Personal Offerings**: The old tradition in ADF is for participants to bring a personal offering of song, poetry or art, to be done in the Grove in honor of the Gods.

11. **The Prayer of Sacrifice**: While offerings may have been being made throughout the rite, at this stage all the energy, worship and aspiration of the participants is gathered up and offered in through the gate to the honored beings of the rite, along with a physical sacrifice. This is the hinge of the rite, after which the energy, which has been being directed into the gate, now turns and begins to flow back in turn.

12. **The Omen**: A simple omen is taken, to determine what sort of blessing the Gods offer in the rite.

13. **Calling for the Blessing**: Participants express their openness to the Gods' blessing, and ask for it to be given.

14. **Hallowing the Waters**: The blessing of the Gods and Spirits is invoked into a cup of ale, water, cider, whiskey, etc. Most commonly this is then drunk by the participants, though in some larger rites it may be sprinkled over all.

15. **Affirmation of The Blessing**: Participants affirm their reception of the blessing, stating again the intention for which they have worked.

16. **Works**: If there are any other specific works for which the blessing has been called, this is the time that they are done.

17. **Final Affirmation**: All again afirm the blessing, and prepare to end the rite.

18. **Thanking the Beings**: All the beings that have been called on in the rite are thanked, in reverse order, from the Deities of the occasion, to the Kindreds, etc.

19. **Closing the Gates**: The Gatekeeper Deity is thanked, and the Gates are declared closed.

20. **Thanking the Earth Mother**: The Earth Mother is thanked, and all leftover offerings or blessing are offered to her.

21. **Statement of Ending**: The rite ends with a clear statement of ending. Sometimes the participants then process out from the Sacred Space.

The Core Order of ADF Ritual for High Days

1. **Initiating the Rite**: May include:
   Musical Signal
   Opening Prayer
   Processional
   Establishing the Group Mind

2. **Purification**: This must take place prior to Opening the Gates

3. **Honoring the Earth Mother**

4. **Statement of Purpose**

5. **(Re)Creating the Cosmos**

6. **Establishing the Sacred Center**

7. **Acknowledging the Three Worlds/Realms**

8. **Acknowledging/Creating the Sacred Fire**

9. **Sacred Center is most commonly represented as Fire, Well & Tree**

10. **Opening the Gate(s)**: Must include a Gatekeeper

11. **Inviting the Three Kindreds**

12. **Key Offerings**: This will commonly include:
    Invitation of Beings of the Occasion
    Seasonal customs as appropriate
    Praise Offerings

13. **Prayer of Sacrifice**

14. **Seeking the Omen**

15. **Calling (asking) for the Blessings**

16. **Hallowing the Blessing**

17. **Affirmation of the Blessing**

18. **Workings (if any)**

19. **Thanking the Beings**

20. **Closing the Gate(s)**

21. **Thanking the Earth Mother**

22. **Closing the Rite**

Items that ADF Rituals Do Not Include

- Elemental Cross Symbolism (the 4 Elements)
- Casting Circles in public ritual
- Calling Watchtowers or Elemental Guardians
- Calling the duotheistic "Lord" and "Lady"
- Acknowledgement of one divine being with power over all
- Blood Sacrifices
- Non Indo-European mythic and deity motifs

Solo High Day Ritual

The Druidic ritual structure is carefully built to allow a worshipper to make contact with the Gods and Spirits and gain a variety of good blessings. As you become comfortable with our systems and symbols you should make an effort to add full ritual to your home High Day celebrations. Full ritual can move your experience from a mere commemoration to a more empowered spiritual event.

All the advice given in our basic guide to ritual applies to solo High Day rites. You will need to choose, make or obtain a Fire, Well and Tree, and arrange a space for them. If you have made a Home Shrine you may choose to do seasonal rites at it. Many find it easiest to arrange the Hallows on an 'altar' or table, while other lay out a cloth and arrange them directly on the floor or ground. Of course if you are working outdoors you may be able to lay you fire directly on the ground or in an iron cauldron, stick your Bile in the soil and place the well at its base. In such cases it can be useful to have a small table to one side to hold the various offerings and props of the rite.

The simplest way to adapt the Order of Ritual to solo High days is to work a simple seasonal charm at the Key Offerings portion of the rite. Most of the Simple Rite of Offering can be worked unchanged, just adding invocations to the proper Deities and Spirits, and any other customs you would like. Our resources offer a number of fully adapted solitary rites, or you can make your own adaptations. Our simple ritual script is easy to adapt at several places.

- The Statement of Purpose should express the basic themes of the high day, name the Gods and Spirits of the rite and declare your intent. If you can write your own statement it will provide an opportunity to clarify your understanding of the High Day.

- The Three Kindreds offerings can be customized in many ways. You can simply call each Kin to "Join me in the rite of (name of High Day)". Some High Days have customs proper to the Dead or the Spirits that might be expressed at this point in the rite.

- The Key Offerings begin with descriptive invocations of the God or Gods of the occasion, and proper offerings for each. In some cases there are additional customs important enough to be set at this point, such as the offering to the Dead at Samhain.

- The Blessing can always be done in the simplest form—hallowing and drinking the Blessing Cup. There are many seasonal customs that are appropriate for the Blessing section of the rite, as well. Customs such as passing between fires at Mayday or the Girdle of Brigid at Imbolc are meant to convey luck and well-being in the coming season.

Book 2

Deepening the Work

Part 8

Lore & Essays

The following essays represent a cross-section of ADF thought and perspective on what modern-day Druids believe–some of the core 'tenets' we hold sacred. The authors each take very individual approaches, yet arrive at a unity of mind, showing that modern Druids seek some of the same truths but in their own personal ways.

Right Action–A Pagan Perspective
DEBORAH KEST

At one time or another, you have probably asked yourself, "Why should I do the right thing?" Like every religion, Our Druidry makes an effort to answer this basic question. One Pagan answer is divine justice: that either in the afterlife or subsequent lives you will have to pay for the bad things you have done and you will be rewarded for the good things. But most of us hope that there is a more substantial, more personal and spiritual reason for doing the right thing than avoiding punishment or garnering rewards. We hope that virtue truly is its own reward.

Living in the modern world, it can be difficult to justify that hope. Too often you hear about bad things happening to good people and criminals getting away with their crimes. It was clear to the ancients, as it is to us, that virtue cannot guarantee happiness. As long as others have the potential to harm you or your loved ones, your well-being is not entirely in your own hands.

Although there are circumstances beyond your control that can stand in your way or harm you and yours, you need not be at the mercy of those forces. Our modern word 'Ethics' comes directly from the Greek ethikos. For all of the Greek philosophers, ethikos was about achieving eudaimonia, literally 'good fate,' or 'with the favor of the gods.' Eudaimonia is usually translated as 'fulfillment,' or 'leading a flourishing life.'

For the ancients, ethics was about having as much control as possible over one's well-being. Although some aspects of eudaimonia are external to the individual, like having sufficient food, warmth, friends and loved ones with whom to interact, most of the elements of a flourishing life are internal goods which are within our control, or at least influence. In northern Pagan cultures these goals were often characterized by the simple triad of 'Health, Wealth and Wisdom.' The ancients called the internal goods that help us to reach these goals excellences or virtues. These concepts are a good place to begin in our effort to find Pagan ways of living.

Each virtue is associated with one of the realms of human activity. To be virtuous in any given realm is to perform that function well. For example, moderation is associated with the realm of the appetites. To be moderate is to satisfy the appetites without overindulgence. Moderation gives you control over your well-being in regards to the appetite because it insures that your needs are met without your becoming a slave to your appetites, or suffering the ill-effects of overindulgence.

Likewise, it is to our benefit to function well in each realm of human activity, not because others will reward us, or because it allows us to avoid punishment, but because it contributes to our eudaimonia. It helps us to lead a more flourishing life, and to a deeper relationship with the gods and goddesses and our fate. One desires to become virtuous because the lack of a virtue hampers one's ability to function well. For example, a lack of courage makes one a slave to one's fears. A lack of hospitality gives one a bad reputation and fewer friends. By consciously choosing to recognize the different realms in which you act, and choosing to act as well as possible in each realm, you will make yourself stronger and wiser-more capable of avoiding bad things happening to you, and more able to respond in a constructive way when they do.

Traditional Pagan ethical systems have a virtue associated with every arena of human functioning. They cover work, play, socializing, conflict resolution, relating to the gods, nurturing and educating children, etc. It is not our purpose here to provide an exhaustive set of virtues, but instead to give a starting list of those excellences important to everyone embracing a value system inspired by the old ways. Some virtues will not appear on this list. That is not to say that they aren't also important, but in the interests of providing a simple starting point, we couldn't include every virtue. The process of examining one's life and becoming more virtuous is ongoing. This list is merely a beginning, for our system and for you. These are not listed in any order of importance. They each interact with all the others, and cannot be ranked one through nine.

Nine Pagan Virtues

1. **Wisdom**: Good judgment, the ability to perceive people and situations correctly, deliberate about and decide on the correct response

2. **Piety**: Correct observance of ritual and social traditions; the maintenance of the agreements, (both personal and societal), we humans have with the Gods and Spirits. Keeping the Old Ways, through ceremony and duty

3. **Vision**: The ability to broaden one's perspective to have a greater understanding of our place/role in the cosmos, relating to the past, present and future

4. **Courage**: The ability to act appropriately in the face of danger

5. **Integrity**: Honor; being trustworthy to oneself and to others, involving oath-keeping, honesty, fairness, respect, self-confidence

6. **Perseverance**: Drive; the motivation to pursue goals even when that pursuit becomes difficult

7   **Hospitality**: Acting as both a gracious host and an appreciative guest, involving benevolence, friendliness, humor, and the honoring of 'a gift for a gift'

8   **Moderation**: Cultivating one's appetites so that one is neither a slave to them nor driven to ill health, (mental or physical), through excess or deficiency

9   **Fertility**: Bounty of mind, body and spirit, involving creativity, production of objects, food, works of art, etc., an appreciation of the physical, sensual, nurturing

Each virtue is the right way to behave in the realm of human functioning with which it is concerned. But it is not always obvious which realm of human functioning is apt. For example, you know that in order to be moderate, you need to cut down on your intake of foods with lots of sugar and fat. But you also know that to be a good guest, you should partake of the food your host has prepared. So you are at a birthday party. Does eating cake fall under the realm of the appetites, or the realm of social situations? Which virtue should you be manifesting, moderation or hospitality? (Or, if you are an alcoholic at a ritual, and you are offered wine for the return flow, which virtue is the issue, moderation or piety?)

There is no single answer to this question, or others like these. Ideally you will manifest both virtues. Perhaps there is some alternative that you can eat that your host has provided, (or a nonalcoholic drink that has been blessed). Or perhaps you can act moderately by partaking of only a small amount. The point is that ethical situations arise on a regular basis without our usually thinking of them as such. The first step to including the virtues in your life is to start noting when you are acting in the realms covered by the nine virtues. When is deliberation in order? What situations call for piety? (Only the eight high day rituals, or sacred times during the day, or whenever you pass a holy object, etc.?) When is vision key?

Once you start noticing the situations in which the different virtues should come to play, the next step is to figure out how to behave more virtuously. Aristotle describes each virtue as a mean between extremes. Courage, for example, is a mean between cowardice, on the one hand, and rashness on the other. To be courageous is neither to shrink from your best action on account of fear, nor to foolishly go into danger when no good is likely to come from your doing so. This means that what is courageous for one person may actually be cowardly for another, and rash for a third, depending on the abilities and situations of the individuals. For a small seven year old to fight a large eight year old bully may be courageous, when it would be cowardly for an adult to act in the same manner, and rash for a four year old to do so.

The key to determining the mean in the case of courage is deliberation about what good is threatened, what options one has to protect that good, and what the likely outcome will be using the different options. The course of action which does not sacrifice the good to fear, when one has a likelihood of protecting it by taking action, is the mean between the extremes of cowardice and rashness, and hence is the courageous one.

But this deliberation is not always easy. Aristotle also recommends that people keep in mind role models, and ask themselves, 'how would this virtuous person act under these circumstances?' Emulating virtuous people helps to inculcate good habits. Another piece of advice that Aristotle offers is to aim at the harder of the two extremes. If you aim at the extreme that is more difficult, it is easier to hit the mean. For example, with courage rashness is more difficult than cowardice. So if you practice ignoring your fear, you will put yourself into the habit of acting courageously more quickly than if you concentrate your energies primarily on careful calculation of risks. With hospitality, being overgenerous is more difficult than being miserly, so you will more quickly develop hospitality by aiming at being extremely charitable than by keeping careful track of who is in whose debt.

Living the Good Life - Pagan Virtue
IAN CORRIGAN

Our Paganism is a constellation of related religions. Like every religion, it's goal is to help humans live successful, happy, productive lives for ourselves and our communities. To that end we work to make ourselves skilled in the ways of life - in gaining wealth, in maintaining health, in growing wise.

Health, Wealth and Wisdom; this is a simple expression of the goals of a fulfilled life in much of Pagan thought. We know that there is no greater good in poverty than in sufficiency - and that sufficiency is true wealth. We know that weakness of mind, body or spirit is always worse than strength - and that strength can be built. We know that our Gods and Goddesses, our Honored Dead, and even the Spirits of the Land wish us well–and that our magic can bring us closer to them. The Old Ways of Europe are filled with wisdom and good counsel that can help us to live well and to do right.

The Pagan movement is inevitably influenced by our experience in modern, Christian-influenced, culture. We may find ourselves living with guilt, anxiety and the feeling that we must live up to a standard of spiritual or moral perfection. Pagan ways can be a powerful antidote to these feelings. For the most part, Pagans do not believe that we must be perfect in our thoughts or actions in order to be acceptable to Spirit, or the Spirits. Our sacred tales are full of examples of heroes, and even Deities, stumbling, erring and enduring the results of error. We learn that we are as nature made us, and that with that making comes the chance to grow and thrive in delightful relation with other beings. The Order of the Worlds gives us the potential to live well, and in most folks the inclination to do good. If we develop ourselves, if we take up the work of Spiritual Practice, with the help of the Spirits, we can realize that potential.

That said, it is also true that overt violations of the virtues were displeasing to the Gods and Spirits and were likely to bring ill upon the violators. Cowardice, refusal of hospitality and other violations of simple goodness are clearly offensive to the Gods, as well as to society. There is nothing mystical in this. The miser is punished in her loneliness and insecurity. The coward dies a thousand deaths in his imagination, then fails in the end. Nature, the Spirits and human wisdom all join to recommend the virtues.

But fear of consequences is never the best argument for the virtuous life. The wisdom of the Ancients grew through thousands of years of accumulated experience. Much more than a system of moral precepts the virtues are the essence of the Pagan way's advice about how to make your life grow and thrive. They help us to build secure homes and families. They guide us toward personal honor and skill. When one's life is lived in harmony, it opens the heart, clears the conscience, and makes possible the flow of spirit that brings magic and inspiration. So we keep the virtues because they offer us a guide to improving our lives and deepening our spirits.

This list of Pagan virtues is not meant to be all-inclusive or final. I present these Nine Virtues as a broad, general outline based on the 'tripartite ideology' (described by George Dumezil) of Indo-European cultures. That model divides those human cultures into the categories of Wise Rulers and Priests, the Warriors and the Providers of Wealth. This is not Pagan theology nor Druidic doctrine. It is a useful way to think about the structure of Pagan cultures and their lore.

As modern people our lives are not as determined by caste and social position as were those of the Ancients. Yet these virtues have much to say to us today. Each of us will, in the course of our lives, have need of the virtues of the Wise, of the Warriors and of the Landkeepers. As in so much of Pagan wisdom, the key is to balance these virtues in yourself and in your life.

Nine Virtues of the Folk

THE WAYS OF THE PROVIDERS

In ancient Europe those who owned and kept the land and herds, those who had the skills of the artisans and makers, those who prepared food and maintained the health of the body, were given due honor.

1. **Industry**: The primary virtue of the makers of wealth is earnest labor in pursuit of bounty and prosperity.

2. **Sensuality**: A central theme of the providers is the power of reproduction, sexuality and pleasure. We affirm that feasting, music and sensual delight are virtues.

3. **Hospitality**: Bounty must be shared. The right of a guest to food and drink, the obligation to share with the clan and with strangers are sacred duties.

THE WAYS OF THE WARRIORS

The need of any people for defense and the ability to stand firm among the strong demanded the presence of warriors. They walked proudly as equals with all others.

1. **Courage**: The primary virtue of the warrior is never to turn away from duty or right action because of fear.

2. **Strength**: The body is the primary weapon and tool of the warrior. It, and the heart and mind, should be able to answer his needs.

3. **Honor**: The warrior's way calls for obedience, mercy, justice and pride. The warrior keeps her oaths, and does right.

THE WAYS OF THE WISE

In ancient cultures the intellectual skills, the keeping of records and lore, the work of philosophy and religion was in the hands of professionals.

1. **Memory**: The primary virtue of the wise rulers is the remembering of history, mythology, legal precedent, and genealogy. Especially, the proper ways of worship and magic must be passed on.

2. **Reason**: The ability to draw conclusions from evidence and precedent provides the objective voice that sees beyond the personal.

3. **Vision**: In order to move forward, a ruler needs innovation, creativity and foresight. The wise seek a developed power of intuition.

Please understand that this classification does not mean that warriors don't need reason, nor farmers courage. In our modern lives we are called to have all of these skills and all of these virtues. We are each called to be warriors, to be producers, to be priest/esses at various times and in various ways. And in each and everyone of these roles all the virtues will be helpful.

Think well on these ideas, and look carefully at how the virtues can be applied in your life. If your goal is to live well and be happy while pursuing your spiritual work, then a virtuous life is the place to begin.

The Nine Noble Virtues of Asatru

Jordsvin (this version)

This rendition of the Nine Noble Virtues with Commentary is public domain. While the Nine Noble Virtues are a modern innovation originated by the Odinic Rite in England, I believe, they are widely used and express well the goals and ethics of our religion.

1. **Courage**: By facing life's struggles with courage, we constantly extend our capabilities. Without courage, nothing else can be done!

2. **Truth**: Blind faith has no place in Asatru. No pie-in-the-sky; we must act in this world as we see it and as it really is rather than calmly wait for the next.

3. **Honor**: We must be true to what we are, and we insist on acting with nobility rather than baseness. Our standards must be banners held high in our hearts.

4. **Fidelity**: We stand true to our faith and our values. Loyalty is the basis for all enduring human activity, and we hold it in the highest esteem.

5. **Hospitality**: The isolation and loneliness of modern life is not necessary. The willingness to share what one has with ones' fellows, especially travelers, is a vital part of our way of life.

6. **Discipline**: We hold to the discipline necessary to fulfill our purpose. We stand willing to exercise the self-control and steadfastness necessary in these difficult times.

7. **Industriousness**: Let us dare to be all that we can be! Let us take risks and taste the richness of life. Passivity is for sheep. We refuse to be mere spectators in life.

8. **Self-Reliance**: We depend on our own strength and character to achieve our goals. We seek only the freedom necessary to our quest, whatever it may be.

9. **Perseverence**: We hold to our path until its completion and are not ashamed to be strong. The cult of the anti-hero will find no support in us, and the gods we follow are not for the weak.

"Cattle die, kinsmen die,
One day you yourself must die.
I know one thing that never dies:
The dead man's reputation."
Havamal–Sayings of the High One

Part 9

Personal Work

The Home Shrine

One of the most traditional ways to begin your relationship with the inner world is to create a personal shrine of worship in your own home. Pagan religion cannot be contained in groves and temples. It is not owned by priestesses or Druids. The reality of Pagan Druidry is found in the hearts of every Pagan who keeps the ways. It is found in every home where the gods and goddesses and spirits are present. So we make a real place in our homes where the powers can be welcomed, a place where we can go to be in their presence, to give offerings and receive blessings. Some may ask 'Aren't the powers present everywhere? Why should we limit them to a single place in our homes?î This question can be answered in several ways.

The old religions did not conceive of the many gods, goddesses and spirits as omnipotent or omnipresent. The powers dwell on the other side, in the many otherworlds, both near to and very distant from our common mortal world. While many of these powers are interested in the lives and well-being of mortals, dwelling close by our common world, Pagan tradition makes it clear that our own participation is required to forge the connection between ourselves and the gods. After all, it is only proper for us to set the table, as it were, for the great ones we hope to welcome.

Tradition makes it clear that the awareness and powers of the gods and spirits manifest through the temples and holy places that mortals create on earth. By making beautiful places, filled with symbolism proper to the work and by filling those places with the devotion of our worship we open a road for the spirits' power.

The Devotional Shrine

The simplest way to begin a home shrine is to place a table or cabinet in a part of your home where it can be private and quiet. There should be enough space for yourself and the members of your household that will use it to sit comfortably for ritual and meditation. You should begin by placing in the shrine symbols of our basic Indo-European Druidic cosmos: fire, well and world-tree or world-mountain. If you have been working simple Druidic rites you will probably have developed a set of tools that you set up and take down at need. You may now wish to use these as your more permanent Shrine Hallows, or you may wish to get another set which you will install and not move if you go outdoors. The home shrine can be constructed as a sacred grove in miniature, a model of the forces that join to open the gates between the worlds.

The fire might best be present as a triple flame, whether a triple-wicked candle or oil flame or three votive candles. White and/or red would be the best colors, though red, white and black, (or green or blue), have much of Indo-European symbolism behind them.

The well should be represented by a simple bowl of water. This can be in the shape of a cauldron if you wish, to partake of all the rich meaning of that symbol.

The world-center symbol on the home altar can be as simple or elaborate as you choose. It is perhaps most proper for it to be of wood: oak, rowan, ash or hazel. A tall stone may also serve, or representations of the pillar tree done in metal or ceramic. Your altar tree or stone can be carved or decorated as you wish.

These simple symbols should become the physical and spiritual center of your shrine. European lore does not give us clear instruction for orienting the shrine. Pagan lore favors either placing the altar in the east, the holy place of the rising sun or in the north, the place of the North Star, center of the sky. The shrine is placed on that wall, so that you sit facing the direction and the altar. Place the tree either against the wall or in the center of the altar area. At its base place the well, with the fire closest to your seat. To these you may wish to add a censer, near the fire, other candles for light, a bowl to hold small offerings and perhaps a bell or chime. From this core symbolism you can begin to add whatever additional patterns appeal to you perhaps patterns drawn from an Indo-European culture who's path you are investigating. If you wish, you may represent the three worlds of land, sea and sky, or symbols proper to an ethnic path. Incense for sky, a shell of saltwater for sea, and a small bowl of salt or clean soil, or a stone or crystal, for the land can fill out the picture.

Of course many or most Pagans will want to include representations or symbols of the gods and goddesses, the ancestors and nature spirits. These you will probably acquire over time, as your own work grows. In fact, the home shrine will serve as a kind of changing and growing map of your growth in the Druid way. As you build a web of worship and relationship with the powers you will rearrange your shrine, adding and subtracting symbols. In time you will have a personal cathedral in a corner of your home, where you can truly commune with the powers and find balance and peace in your soul.

Three Bowls and a Stick:
Creating a Home Shrine on a Budget

Michael J. Dangler

I started work on my Dedicant Program as soon as I joined ADF. At the time, I was a college student living in an apartment with two people who did not share my religious beliefs. Since we all know that 'college student' = 'poor', I won't try to describe my economic situation too much.

I didn't set up an altar immediately. In the original DP, there was no order to the whole thing, and the Home Shrine was actually near the back of the material. It wasn't until I heard Skip Ellison (our Archdruid at that time) speak at Summerland on daily worship rites that I started constructing my own Home Shrine.

Skip's workshop wasn't really on altars, but he did mention sacred spaces in the home, and he described his altar quite thoroughly. Immediately after his workshop, I started to take notes on what I wanted in an altar.

I'm a firm believer that an altar should reflect the practicalities of your situation. Since I hadn't told my parents I was Pagan, if they came by, they'd see my altar, so I wanted something I could put away, which is in pretty direct defiance of what the DP tells you to do. I had the added worry of two white cats, which means that I couldn't set up a permanent altar anywhere within their reach, and I couldn't use a black altar cloth (or any other color) due to their fantastic ability to fling the hair they shed to the oddest corners of the room.

My absolute poverty as a college student was another thing to overcome. The Archdruid had shown us his traveling altar, and he had some nice things. There is also the section about the Home Shrine in the DP material that suggested many things for the altar: a cauldron for the well, a triple-wick candle for the fire, and a carved piece of wood for the tree. 'The home shrine is a sacred grove in miniature,' the DP said. Representations of the deities could be added, as could symbols for land, sea, and sky. That's a lot to purchase on a budget. I didn't even have a table to put this stuff on!

Well, I shopped for days to find a triple-wick candle that was unscented, and I couldn't find one in my town, anywhere. I gave up on that and decided to grab three votive candles and use those. I was too poor to buy a cauldron, so I found an old Tupperware bowl and used that as my well. Instead of a real altarcloth, I used a white dishcloth (still in use, I might add!). I used some Dixie cups that I had cut in half for offering cups, until I found a couple more Tupperware bowls. As the finishing touch, I took a stick and stood it upright on the altar, and this became the tree. My altar was, simply put, three bowls and a stick.

I initially had the altar set up on a set of drawers, too low for me to stand in front. The top drawer was reserved for my altar stuff, and everything had its place in there. It has since been moved to be permanently visible, set into the top shelf of a bookshelf, due mainly to relaxed relationship issues and one less roommate.

As time progressed, I have replaced things. At an after-Christmas sale at Target, I picked up a greeting card holder shaped like a Christmas tree that I use as my tree ($4). I bought a small cauldron at a local Pagan shop for $9 to replace my first Tupperware bowl. I've bought some statues from Sacred Source, which represent the only serious monetary investment into this altar so far. My first votive candles lasted a year and a half before they needed replacing.

In short, the Home Shrine doesn't need to be perfect, nor does it need to be expensive, pretty, or any other adjective. While it would be ideal if it were permanent, certain living situations might cause problems with this. I would suggest that if it cannot be permanent, you at least set it up in the same place each time you use it, with the same altar configuration. If you're living in temporary housing of any sort, something as simple as three bowls and a stick might be ideal. Take your life into consideration, and consider the impact this altar will have on it: do your parents come over often, and if so, do they know/care that you're Pagan? Do you have children or cats that might knock things off the altar? This is your altar, so do what you will with it.

As food for thought, remember that nothing limits you to only one altar, either!

Hallowing the Home Shrine

The householder must gather water from three sources. If possible this should include consecrated Wells, but any clean, natural source will do. The Three Waters should be combined, and kept ready in a bottle or jug. She must also gather three sacred woods. The strongest choices might be Oak, Rowan and Hazel, though the householder may choose as she will. The amount of wood need only be enough for a small fire in the ritual 'hearth', that has been chosen for the Shrine. If the Shrine is a small table, and the hearth is candles and a censer, then the woods may be rendered into small shavings or even powder. If you wish, you may make a 'kindling incense', thus:

Duile Incense

- 3 Herbs: Vervain - 1 part; Mistletoe - 1 pt; Mugwort - 1 pt
- 3 Flowers: Rose - 2 pts; Saffron - 2 pts; Lavendar - 2 pts;
- 3 Woods: Oak, Rowan, Hazel—combine 1/3 part of each

File or grind the wood to powder, and be certain that it is very dry. Pound all together with orris root and moisten it with rose and lavender oils.

The Householder must prepare his Shrine. The central feature of the Shrine should be a set of simple Hallows. A water-cauldron (the Coire Tobar), a 'hearth' (Tinteann) that might allow a tiny open fire, or candles and a censer, and a small pillar or stone to stand as the World-Tree or Mountain make up the Home Hallows. No other items are mandatory for a basic Shrine, but you may wish to add a cloth to cover the table, extra illumination, bowls to hold offerings, a bell or chime and, of course, images or tokens of the Gods and Spirits. Such tokens can be placed even on a new Shrine, before you have built personal alliances with the Kindreds.

As you prepare for the Rite, the Coire and Tinteann will be empty. You will bring your Triple Water and Sacred Fire in simple bowls, to be transferred onto the Shrine. If possible, you should try to fetch a spark from some already hallowed Fire to light your own. One simple way to do this is to light a stick of incense from a Sacred Fire, and keep transferring it to another stick (perhaps using matches) until you can get it home to a candle or Tineann.

When you have gathered all of these things, bring them to the place where you will make your Shrine. Set up the table with its cloth. If possible arrange the Shrine so that you are facing east, with the Hallows in the center before you. Arrange any other items as you wish. The Water is to one side in a bowl, the Coire empty. The Fire is prepared in the new Tinteann, but not yet lit. If you have brought a spark from another Fire, it is to one side in a small candle or incense stick. Arrange a seat before the Shrine that allows you to easily reach all the tools of the rite.

The Working

Settle yourself in your seat, begin a breathing pattern, and work the Two Powers as your skill allows, perhaps using the Kindling Charm. If you like, ring a bell nine times to signal the formal opening of the rite.

Give the Opening Invocation:

The world is in me,
And I am in the world
The spirit in me is the spirit in the world

By Eye and by Hand and by Tongue
My will is the will of the world.
And this is my will, to make these things a Shrine of Druidry, a seat of
wisdom, my own Hearth, and the Well of the Spirit. Biodh se amhlaidh!

Take up the bowl of the Triple Water and sprinkle the Shrine and each of the tools, as you say:

By the holy Power of the Deep; The Waters of the Dark, the secret Well,
Be free of every ill or every bane; Washed clean by magic's might, as I do will.

Take up the incense, or light incense from the flame, and pass each object through its smoke, saying:

By the shining Power of the Sky; The Fire of Druidry, the Heaven's Light
Let every ill or bane now flee away; By my word and will, and magic's might.

End the cleansing, saying:

By the might of the Waters and the Light of the Fire
Be you cleansed and blessed! Be you made whole and holy!
By my word and by my will, so be it!

Take up the bowl of water, and pour the water into the Tobar while speaking a proper briocht, such as:

O Cauldron of the Deep Power, I bring you into my service, and place you in my Shrine. I set you
in the Center to be a part of the Sacred Center, and I charge you:

You are the gate of the earth
The deep way, the holy mouth
Anu's cunny

Chorus: By the ladies of waters
By the lords of waters
By the powers under the earth
I thank you for the sacred waters.

You are the eye of the earth
Mirror of seeing, gate of visions
Spring of wisdom (repeat chorus)

You are the mouth of the earth
Sustainer of life, receiver of gifts
Giver of blessings (repeat chorus)

Using a candle, transfer fire into the ritual Fire, lighting the small fire or candles. Speak as is proper, perhaps:

O Hearth of the Power of Fire, I bring you into my service, and place you in my Shrine. I set you
in the Center to be a part of the Sacred Center, and I charge you:

I kindle the sacred fire
In the presence of the shining ones
In the presence of the gods of fire
In the presence of the goddesses of fire
Without malice, without envy,
Without jealousy, without fear,
Without terror of anything under the sun

Personal Work

And the holy son of the mother to shield me.
Oh sacrificed and sacrificer
Kindle you in our hearts
A flame of wit and heart and strength
To bear my offerings and my words
To the gods, the dead and the sidhe
Oh you who aid us all
Friend and foe, high and low
I call you to be in this Hearth
And bring to me your blessing.

Place the Tree or Stone in its place between the Fire and Well, and conjure it with a proper charm, such as:

O Pillar of the Temple, I bring you into my service, and place you in my Shrine. I set you in the Center to be a part of the Sacred Center, and I charge you:
Rooted deep within the land, Crowned above the sky
The tree is planted in my soul, To grow between the worlds.
Bile I name you, as of old, Center of All Things
Boundary of boundaries, Hold fast my work, my soul, my Grove

Take a moment to contemplate the whole symbol of the Three Hallows together, and say:

The Fire, the Well, the Sacred Tree, Flow and flame and grow in me
In Land, Sea and Sky, below and on high, Thus are these Hallows claimed and hallowed!

Take up the Tobar and sprinkle the four corners of the Shrine-table, saying:

What was cleansed, now let it be filled. Oh Shrine of my Druidry, receive the Dark Strength of the Underworld. Be you the soil in which the seed of my spirit grows.

Cense the four corners of the Shrine-table with incense lit from the Fire, saying:

What is cool, now let it be warmed. O Shrine of my Druidry, receive the bright power of the heavens. Be you the sun that brings my spirit to fruit.

Replace all in their proper places on the Shrine. Strengthen the Two Powers in yourself, and charge the whole Shrine again, saying:

Mighty, Noble and Shining Ones
Here is my Shrine.
Let it be a Seat of Power, and Ark of Wisdom,
A Font of Love between myself and the Gods and Spirits.
Let it grow as I grow, change as I change,
As I speak with the Spirits, and they with me.
Let the Fire be bright in it
Let the Waters be deep in it
As I walk my Path.
So be it!

Renew your peace and center one final time, and say:

The Fire, the Well, the Sacred Tree
Flow and flame and grow in me
I give thanks to all beings who have witnessed or aided in this work,
And declare this rite ended.
So be it!

Druidic Mental Training

Like many of the world's religions, Druidry emphasizes the importance of training the mind. The practices of meditation and trance, relaxation, concentration and vision are the basic skills of both magic and religion. They bring myth and ritual to life, deepen devotion and help us to comprehend our own souls.

The work of schooling the mind is a lifetime's task. The elder Druids spent as long as 20 years to make finely-tuned instruments of their minds. Most Pagans may never choose that kind of focus on mind-training. Still there are important basic techniques that can be valuable to every Pagan who wishes to clarify her own mind and deepen her interaction with the Inner Worlds.

We offer these exercises to our members in hope that they will be effective steps on their personal path. Our Druidry is a path of ceremony and seership, of devotion and of self-knowledge, and of inner vision. The techniques given here are tools to be employed in your devotions and rites, in the work of establishing a relationship with the Gods and Spirits. Some of you will find them important to your personal path, but even if these skills tax your patience, everyone will benefit from the effort of learning the basics.

Regularity and privacy are two of the basic principles that bring success in mental training. Privacy allows you to truly relax and detach your mind from its social surrounding and programs. If you choose to begin practical spiritual work, you must consciously choose to set aside some few minutes each day to tend only to yourself, and later to the Gods and Spirits. This tells the mind something important. It speaks of the value of spiritual work - that your own soul has needs and value.

Regularity is important in learning any skill, and religion and magic are no different. All teachers begin by asking for daily practice of the techniques they mean to teach. Human nature as it is, some students will heed this advice and some will not. Nevertheless, there is a simple formula at work. Daily practice yields results seven times faster than weekly practice! These techniques will bring results if followed, but every student will have his own life, her own issues, that may bring unique challenges. So we hope you will do as much as you can, when you can. Though regularity is best, any practice is better than none!

Getting Started

Tradition teaches that it is best to choose a special place in which to practice your first mental training. For us that will be our Home Shrine, where you work your personal devotions, though finding a quiet outdoor place is also very valuable. You should choose a restful, secluded place, where you can be away from telephones, doorbells and other interruptions.

Many people prefer to sit cross legged, and learn meditation seated crosslegged, in the fashion of yogis, or Celtic diners. This has the advantage of being quite portable, and suited for outdoor work. If possible a thick cushion or low seat should be used, high enough to raise the tailbone above the ankles. This prevents the feet from falling asleep so readily. Others prefer to use an upright chair, though this should be one that encourages a straight spine.

The first technique is the base on which all mental training rests.

The Complete Breath

The Wise know that to control the breath is to control the mind. To begin, sit comfortably, with your spine straight. Your tailbone should be higher than your ankles, your hands resting loosely on your lap or on the arms of your chair. Your eyes may be slightly open, or closed. You then begin a pattern of rhythmic breathing.

Proper breath comes from the diaphragm. When you inhale, your lower abdomen should expand, as though you were pulling air into the bottom of the lungs. Then fill the rest of the lungs, expanding the chest. When the breath is held, do not close the throat. Keep the diaphragm and chest expanded to let the air rest in the lungs. Exhaling reverses the process, emptying the chest then raising the diaphragm by pressing the belly toward the backbone. Again, the breath is held out of the body by the muscles of the chest and belly, not by closing the throat.

Tradition offers several patterns for rhythm of the breath. Many people like the classic 4/4 pattern –in for four beats, hold for four beats, out for four beats, hold for four beats. The speed of the rhythm is up to you. A little practice will allow you to find a pace that is comfortable, neither too slow nor too fast. Some prefer a pattern with shorter holds, perhaps in-4, hold-2, out-4, hold-2.

If you are beginning meditation, your daily practice can be the practice of the Complete Breath, perhaps practiced as a preliminary to your devotions, until it is habitual and comfortable. You will find that it shades naturally into the core techniques of trance and meditation.

Basic Trance

As you sit breathing comfortably, repeat the count of your breath silently to yourself. Let this simple reality be your 'mantra'. Much has been made of mantras and their secret powers. Some of that is true lore, but some is simply sleight-of-mind. For this basic work we can use the simple repetition of the count as a way to focus and relax the body and mind.

As you sit, breathing and counting your breaths, thoughts will arise naturally, and your body will find ways to become tense. The first goal of the practice is to remember to allow your body to relax, and to allow thoughts to arise, float naturally through your awareness and then disperse like smoke. At first the tendency will be to begin 'thinking about' your thoughts, your mind attaching to them in the ordinary way. This is what you hope to avoid. By gently returning the focus to counting the breath, common thoughts can be released and allowed to flow away. So count the breaths, and any time you find yourself focused on any train of thought, or find your shoulders or face, etc., becoming tense, simply breath, relax, and return your attention to counting your breaths.

When you have observed your thought for a time, you may choose to imagine that your thoughts are like sparks of light, like fireflies flashing or embers spinning by. You may then begin to will those lights to go out. Extinguish each light as it arises. Feel your body grow settled and relaxed, and your mind grow darker, calmer and more peaceful. The goal is to find a state in which your body is comfortable and relaxed, and your mind is calm and relatively still - at least able to allow disturbing ideas to flow easily through, without disturbing other work.

With practice you will have longer periods in which you sit comfortably, without becoming attached to any thought. In time you will be able to sit at ease, steady and firm, as the flow of your thoughts goes by. This simple practice of observing the thoughts has great value. It relieves stress and frees the mind from worry. It attunes the body to itself and its rhythms, and brings peace to the soul.

This basic mental poise, this basic state of relaxed alertness is the blank slate on which we mean to write the ways and patterns of our Pagan paths. It allows us access to our own minds, allows us to build the inner temples and paths that bring us into contact with the Gods and Spirits. It can proceed and conclude any ritual, and is the door to deeper trance, vision, and inner devotional work. It relieves stress, frees the mind from worry for a time and creates an open, receptive state for worship and magic. It has real value as a practice in itself, but it is also a basis on which other techniques are built. The work of spiritual practice often requires periods of focused awareness, when we hope to maintain specific thoughts and images in our mind. By learning to allow common thought to slide through our awareness we can better apply our will to focusing the mind on the images and invocations of our devotions and offerings.

Visualization and Energy Work

Once you have mastered the basic trance–that is, once you can sit quietly, with both body and mind relaxed but alert–you can move on to the work of visualization and energy. Both visualization and energy work require the ability to produce mental experiences that seem to be sensory, to the mind. In energy work we use imagination to produce the feeling of energy flowing through the body, and in visualization we use it to produce mental images. Of course all the other senses are also employed in producing a fully-realized vision–inner hearing, touch, etc. play their part.

The Two Powers script given here is an example of using vision skills to produce the feeling of energy flow in the body. We build the feel of the cool earth-power, the warm light, the tingle or thrill of the flow, the vision of the fire flowing in us. Such a script should really be experienced as a guided exercise, at first. This often happens in our public rituals, but solitary students may need to resort to recording the script in their own voice, at a stately, gentle pace.

We have also provided basic scripts for beginning vision-journeying. The skills of sending a vision-eye into the edges of the otherworld, using self-guided imagery, is a somewhat more advanced technique that has great value.

So begin the work of mental training and keep to its discipline as well as you can. Regular practice and an open heart will always produce results in this most basic of meditation practices.

The Two Powers

This is a basic meditation intended to link the Druid's spirit and flesh to the currents of Earth and Sky. It is based on methods that have become known in Pagan work as 'grounding and centering'. All these methods are meant to connect the student to spiritual powers in the cosmos, and to provide balanced channels of flow for those powers in the personal soul. Some form of this technique should precede almost any work of worship or magic. The Two Powers model is based on core concepts in Indo-European lore, but is not, by any means, the only vision or mythic model useful in our Druidry.

The work begins by seating yourself, or standing, in a comfortable position at your meditation seat. Here follows a script for a version of the Two Powers work. You should read through the script until you are familiar with its pattern, or perhaps even read it onto a tape for the first several exercises. Soon, with practice, you will know the basic order, and be able to proceed from memory. The best practice is to memorize the sequence of images, but this is made much easier by a few repetitions with spoken guidance.

THE SCRIPT

"Begin, O seeker of wisdom, with your breath…breathe deeply, from your belly…in…and out…make your body comfortable…stretch if you need to, settle in place…and focus on your breath…observe your breath as it flows in and out of your body…and with each breath, allow your body to relax…let your breath carry away tension from your flesh.. relaxing your feet and legs…letting your belly soften and relax…breathing away tension from your shoulders and arms…from your neck…relaxing your face and mouth, your eyes…with each breath your body becoming warmer, comfortable and relaxed…your mind alert and prepared for magic…

Now, with your body still and calm, imagine that from your feet, or the base of your spine, roots begin to grow downward…roots reaching and growing into the earth, down through soil and stone…deepening and spreading…reaching to touch the waters under the Earth…the Earth current…the dark, cool, magnetic power that nourishes and sustains life…as your roots touch this current it is drawn in and up toward your body…your breath draws the Earth power upward…into your body…the invisible, magnetic power fills your legs, energizing and strengthening…waters rise from the earth, into your legs…rising…into your loins…and pooling in your loins, a cauldron of Earth power…You breathe the power upward... rising from the earth, through your loins, rising up your spine... into your heart... pooling and filling a cauldron in your heart with healing, restoring energy... power rising from the deep, through your loins, through your heart... rising up your spine and into your head... filling a cauldron of wisdom and vision behind your eyes... and rising still, filling all your body and flowing out again through the crown of your head... through your hands... flowing out around your body and back into the earth... the power under the Earth flows in you... grounding you in the source of life...

Now imagine the sky overhead... The sun and moon and, far beyond them, the stars... imagine a single star at the center of the sky, shining directly over your head... the center of your inner sky, your own pole-star... see a flash of light shining down from that star... streaming down between moon and sun... gold, silver and blue-white light... the bright, warm, electric power of the sky... the light touches your head, filling and illuminating the cauldron like sun on still water... shining from above... filling your head with warm, awakening power... flowing down into your heart... warming the cauldron... shining down through head and heart, illumining the waters... downward to reach your loins... The cauldron shines with sky power in your loins... Tingling, electrical light in head, heart and loins... the light flows downward into Earth, and you are shining and flowing with the mingled powers of Earth and sky... the raw material of magic... the chaos of potential and the world order...

These powers are balanced in you... yours to shape and use... always with you in some degree... But for now, allow the powers to recede... waters to the Earth, light to the sky... knowing that each time you attune to them you become more attuned, more at one with the powers... breath deep... and allow your awareness to return to your common senses... as you open your eyes..."

The Inner Work of the Simple Devotional

Visualization, Energy Work and Aspiration

[1] Be seated at your Shrine, and make your body comfortable.

[2] Begin rhythmic breathing, in whatever pattern is comfortable for you.

[3] Spend a few moments finding a relaxed physical feeling and a quiet, focused mind. Say:

I am here to honor the Gods
I am here to remember the Elder Spirits
I am here to keep the Ways of Druidry

[4] Perform the Two Powers meditation, or whatever Grounding and Centering exercise is effective for you.

[5] Feel the flow of the Fire and Water, Sky and Earth Powers in the self. See your Shrine Hallows before you, symbolizing those powers. Feel your spine to be like the World Tree, or the Pillar in the Temple, or the Mountain of the Gods as you say:

The Fire, the Well, the Sacred Tree
Flow and flame and grow in me.
I span between the Earth and Sky,
Rooted deep and crowned high.

[6] Visualize the curve of the world stretching out from you in all directions, the Land with its green life, the deep sea, the overarching sky. Spend a moment to feel yourself firmly in the center of the triskel, seated with the World Pillar in your body and spirit. Anoint yourself with the Three Worlds symbols and say:

The primal Sea around me
The shining Sky above me

The holy Land beneath me
The Order of the Worlds stands firm
Around me and within my soul.

[7] Into this visualized cosmos come the Gods and Spirits. In whatever way is true for you, see the Gods, and the Ancestors, and the Landspirits informing and inhabiting this cosmos of Land, Sea and Sky, Heavens and Underworld. To all theses divine beings, offer your aspiration - your seeking to know them, and be known by them, your affection for them and your delight in their presence. Make your offerings, saying:

I offer my offerings…
…In the eye of the Mothers who bore me
…In the eye of the Fathers who quickened me
…In the light of the fire
and the sight of the Powers

Accept me, I pray, as your kin and ally
…Mighty and beloved Dead
…Wild Ones, Nobles of the Land
…Eldest, Wisest, Shining Ones

Accept from me this offering
That your power
inspire and instruct me
That your power
heal and sustain me
That your power
preserve and defend me
Each shade and light
Each day and night
Each hour in blessing
This I ask, and give you this due honor!

[8] Allow the whole vision of the rite to be present in your mind. Again, know the presence of the Light and Shadow, the Land, Sea & Sky, the Gods, Dead & Spirits. Continue to offer your aspiration along with your physical offerings and be alert for any feeling of response from within your vision.

[9] When you feel that you are finished, let yourself feel gratitude to all the beings that may have been affected by your work, open your heart in love for the Worlds and the Kindreds, and give the Great Blessing:

I offer my thanks to the Mother of All.
I offer my thanks to the Gods, Dead and Spirits.
May the Three Sacred Kins
Bring joy to all beings, and renew the ancient wisdom.
To the Earth, Sea, and Sky I offer my thanks
May Wisdom, Love and Power
Kindle in all beings, and renew the ancient wisdom.
To the Fire, Well and Tree I offer my thanks.
May the ancient wisdom be renewed,
And may all beings know peace, joy and happiness
In all the worlds.
So be it!

Passing the Mist

This trance-vision exercise is intended to allow the Druid to send a vision-body from the material world in which the ritual is set into an imaginal location closer to the Otherworld. In such an environment the Gods and Spirits are more able to speak to the Druid, and the Druid is better able to send her voice into the Inner Realms.

Seat yourself comfortably at your Hallows, back straight, perhaps braced against a tree.

Perform the Two Currents centering, or renew and strengthen your Earth and Heavens contacts.

Feel the cool Earth Power and the hot Sky Power meet in your head, meet in your heart, meet in your loins. Gaze upon your own Fire, Well & Tree, and understand the Two Powers to be flowing in them as it is in you.

And in the meeting-places, where Fire and Water meet, feel the mingling of the Powers begin to produce a Mist - the streams of vapor pouring out of your Hallows, flowing out from the roots of the Tree, where Fire and Water meet.

Visualize the Mist gathering and thickening, beginning to accumulate around you, filling your Grove. Even as the Powers are meeting in your Hallows, and the Mist flows from them, you may perceive the Mist arising from you, yourself, from the meeting of the Two Powers in your spirit.

The Mist gathers, growing thicker, and collecting around your feet... around your hips and loins... around your arms and chest. It grows thick and opaque, and rises, at last, to surround your head.

With your eyes closed, envision the Wizard's Mist as it surrounds you... see it grey and silver and white, sometimes glistening, sometimes shadowed, growing thicker, warm and comforting.

This is the Mist of the Between... the place of neither/nor... neither waking nor sleeping, neither in the common world or in the Otherworld... a place where journeying may happen... a place of unknown possibility... rest here for a while... rest in meditation as your mind holds the presence of the swirling Mist of the Border...

Now, seated in the Mist, it is time to begin... in your imagination's eye... in your Inner Vision... not with your physical body... Stand up... Use your body in vision... brace yourself... and rise up from where you are seated... feel your point-of-view rise with your head... holding your point-of-view behind your imagined eyes... You stand up in your vision body... you take a step forward... and stand in the Mist...

You may, if you wish, look down at yourself... Though there is no need... you feel the presence of your hands... of your body upright... as the Mist swirls all around you...

Now it is your task to part the Mist and move into the vision reality of the land on which you began... bring to mind the physical forms of your Hallows... let your memory recall your Fire, Well and Tree before you... see their shape and color... recall their nature...

In vision, reach your hand before you, and draw a deosil spiral, from center out to edge, in the Mist before you... focused on your goal image, see the Mist swirl where you draw... and see it begin to part...

Now the Mist begins to thin... as though blown by an unfelt wind... now, with memory and will... you see the scene resolve before you... the Inner form of your Hallows, the Inner Nemeton, revealed in its Otherworld form... elements of the same scene that you left when you called the Mist... see it resolve in your Inner Eye... as the Mist clears around you... revealing the Inner reflection of the ritual space...

You behold the Inner World resolving before you... you see the details more clearly now...

The Inner World is brighter, but perhaps less 'in focus'... it glimmers and wavers, resolving only when you gaze directly at a scene... sometimes resolving sharply, all on its own...

In your vision body, turn and look around you... turn to your right... and to your left... turn at last and look behind you... you are aware of your body, seated in the common world... You take note of its position... as you look at the Inner World around you...

(If this is your first experience of passing the Mists, or if anything doesn't feel right about the experience, this is as far as you should go. Skip to the return instructions.)

If all feels well to you, you may wish to walk out into the Inner... for these first experiments, remaining near to your physical body... your Sacred Fire, lit before you, will always be visible to you... always be a beacon for returning... no matter how far you roam...

So, for a time, explore the Inner Land in which you find yourself... look at the plants and stones... look round to see the presence of birds, beasts or beings... but for now, do not seek to interact with them... only observe...

...and, after a time, turn and look for the glint of your Sacred Fire... and return to the place where you can dimly glimpse your body...

The Return

Standing in vision before your body... turn, and step backward into the space where your body is sitting... raise your spirit-hand before you... and make a tuathal triskel in the air before you... and see the Mist draw around you againÖ sit down into your body... and see the Mist rise around you... renew your center... feel the Earth and Sky Powers meeting in your flesh... as the Mist rises around you... you are again in the place between...

Remember your body, and, as the Mist parts again, breathe deep... feel the air flow in your lungs... the blood course in your veins... open your eyes, and know that your spirit has returned fully to your flesh... stretch... and be finished with the trance.

Part 10

Walking the Path

We begin our exposition of the ritual work of Druidry with the intentions of our rites, both the limited and specific goals of any one rite, and the greater meaning present in the order of ritual itself. Every rite performed in this order partakes of three 'meta-programs' of spiritual intent.

The Intentions of Druidic Ritual

To Rectify and Empower the Souls of the Worshippers

The most consistent and personal result of sincere participation in ritual is the creation or strengthening of the patterns of our spiritual cosmos in the souls of individual worshippers. Whether this pattern exists innately in all people or whether we must create it there through our work, it is strengthened and deepened by repeated meditation and ritual acknowledgment.

The lore of Indo-European Paganism assumes that the inner worlds and otherworlds reflect and are reflected by our manifest world. By making our simple physical images of cosmic order, our sacred grove, we draw these inner realities closer to the manifest world. When we in turn meditate on these symbols, recreating them in vision in ourselves, they become a kind of map that allows a clearer, more ordered understanding of the contents of our minds and hearts.

Druidry is not focused exclusively on 'the light' or 'the heavens', nor do we value the inner or spiritual world more highly than the manifest world or the contents of our souls. We understand the inner world to be integrated with the physical world, and hold both to be equally holy. We use ritual to manifest the powers of the inner world in our common world. By using our art, craft and skill we create physical and spiritual events that reflect and manifest inner realities.

When a Pagan successfully integrates these patterns, they act as a kind of realignment for the mind and heart. Even if we assume that these patterns are inborn in us all, it is clear that the stresses of everyday life in our secular culture can leave us uncentered and disoriented. Thoughtful, intentional participation in ritual is one of the key answers to this modern alienation.

To Serve the Gods, Goddesses and Spirits

In contrast with much of Paganism, our Druidry tends to adopt a theology that views the many powers described in tales and lore as independent, living entities. We reject, in general, theories that view the powers as projections of our own minds, or as thought-forms created by human worship or as archetypes in the collective unconscious. Instead we prefer the traditional understanding of the nature of the gods, goddesses and spirits and of humanity. We can describe this understanding as having three parts.

First, humans are powers in and of themselves. We have innate abilities to shape thoughts, words and things just as do the powers, and are capable of magic even without their aid. The greatest of us can be the equal of nearly any being, and all of us are able to exercise a degree of spiritual authority according to our talent and skill.

Second, we know that while there are many spirits that may be weaker than us, there are many that are vastly more powerful. Many of these mighty ones are connected with the very maintenance of the life and health of ourselves and our land.

Third, in order to live well, we need the blessing of these great powers. This is obtained through worship, sacrifice and attunement. By thus bringing ourselves into contact with these beings we allow them to be reflected to some degree in our own souls, bringing their blessing into our lives.

All traditional Paganism says that it is proper to give gifts of our own skill, art and substance to the powers. The ancients offered carefully crafted objects of precious metal and wood as well as fruits of labor, food and drink to those they worshipped, and it is proper for us to do the same today. We must assume that the spirits want and need these gifts just as we need their blessings. So by our rites of worship we feed the powers and acknowledge our mutual interdependence with them.

This worshipful approach can help us to avoid the inflation of the personal ego that has been the besetting error of the Western magical tradition. We do not teach that we are 'God' or identical with God or the Universe. Rather we acknowledge that each of us is one element in the great dance of being. If we are skilled and talented we may come to a very great spiritual power and understanding, perhaps even becoming a god or goddess. Yet even the greatest of the powers worships and sacrifices to the other gods, goddesses and spirits. The web of mutual obligation never ends nor would we wish it to, for it is the thing that sustains all existence.

To Bless the Folk and the Land

Our Druidry is neither meant to be humble, one-sided giving to the powers nor vague, feel-good spirituality. Pagan religion hopes always to provide real benefit to the community it serves. In traditional lore this is often expressed as three great goods - health, wealth and wisdom. Again, Paganism does not reject the things of this material world in favor of spiritual things. Every human life needs a balance of physical well-being, sufficient goods and mental and spiritual growth. We expect our religious rites to be practical aids toward these goals.

The order of ritual contains several intrinsic benefits for all who join in wholeheartedly. First, as mentioned, is the establishment or strengthening of the cosmic patterns in the soul, making us more firmly grounded and more effectively centered. Second is the deepening of our contact with the gods, goddesses and spirits. As Pagans, we work to establish personal relationships with individual deities, members of the faery tribes and with our own ancestors and the elder wise ones. When we participate in the offerings to the three Kindreds, we have the opportunity to call to our own allies among the powers, thus strengthening our personal magic. The third source of blessing is the blessing itself, which we call the 'return flow'.

The worshipper should formulate carefully what she desires to receive from any rite, and everyone should expect real results, real life-changes from the blessing and drinking of the blessing cup.

As modern Pagans, we have a special duty to heal and defend the land itself. Our holy Earth has been deadened by centuries of loveless abuse, and it should be part of every Druid rite to appeal to, waken and honor the land that upholds our work. Our order of ritual gives us several opportunities. The first is at the Earth Mother offering, when the local goddess of the land, and/or the Earth Mother of the chosen pantheon is honored. The second is at the nature spirits offering, when the tribes of spirits who enliven the area are worshipped, and the third could be at the blessing itself, when a portion of the blessing might be poured on the Earth, so that the land may share in the results of the work.

Practical Considerations

Having discussed the theoretical bases of our work we may now examine practical considerations in choosing your intent and goal for a Druidic rite.

Pantheon and Patrons

The primary outer purpose of most Druid ritual is to worship the powers, the deities and spirits. In much of the Pagan revival powers from a variety of cultures and systems are often worshipped together. While this happens in Druidry as well, we encourage the choice of a single cultural pantheon for each individual rite. This gives focus to the rite, ensures that the powers are in harmony and encourages the gaining of lore about ancient Pagan cultures. So the first step in designing a Druidic rite is to decide within which cultural complex the rite will be done.

Of course, any system that chooses to call itself 'Druidry' will have a strong interest in the ways of the Pagan Celts. We are no exception. However ¡r nDra'ocht FÈin is open to all Indo-European cultures, and we have folks working in Norse, Hellenic, Baltic and Slavic systems as well.

Of course, the strongest element in this choice will be your own interest in and dedication to a particular pantheon. If you are working alone you can simply use your own first choice of pantheon, but groups will need to reach a consensus. Choosing a single cultural paradigm allows a group to deepen and strengthen its magical connection with those powers, while experimentation broadens experience and encourages research. The choices are yours.

Once you have determined the pantheon for your rite, you must also choose the particular powers to whom the central offerings and callings will be made. This decision will be based on the occasion and the magical intent of the rite. Most often, these patron powers are a pair of deities, a goddess and a god, though rites can also be offered to the ancestors or the spirits of the land.

Those working alone, or in a small group that shares a focus, may find a desire to worship only one or two deities from a single pantheon or personal patron deities. This is fine, but it is important to include the broader company of powers from the pantheon from which these patrons are drawn. To this end, our order of ritual requires offerings to several categories of deity, reducing the problem of focusing on personal deities alone.

The Occasion of the Rite

Seasonal Rites: Ár nDraíocht Féin has formally adopted the modern Neopagan calendar of eight seasonal holy days. These are, of course, the four astronomical days, i.e., the solstices and equinoxes combined with the so-called fire festivals of the Celts - Samhain, Imbolg, Beltaine and Lughnasadh. We have not established a specific set of symbols or mysteries for these occasions. The form and content of each is up to you, though we will provide scripts from which you may draw inspiration. Again, your own research and meditation will be the best guide to the proper symbols for each feast.

ADF is not attempting to revive any of the ancient Pagan religions of the cultures we study. We base our work on authentic ancient lore and effective modern magical and religious technique, realizing that we are creating a new religion for ourselves as modern people. Thus, we use the standard dates and core symbols of the modern Pagan calendar, fitting various ethnic traditions into this pattern. While a grove may choose to perform rites based on a specific ethnic tradition on dates different from the core calendar, the eight core holidays must be offered to the community.

Rites of Passage: As in any religion, Pagans hallow the important occasions of our lives with ritual. Births, child blessings, coming of age ceremonies, religious vocations, weddings and funerals can all be proper occasions for our rites.

Personal Magical Work: The ADF order of ritual has been evolved mainly for public worship with medium to large groups. Using the order for small and individual workings is quite possible, but may require some variation. Below we provide a simple script that can be used as a stepping off point for individual and small-group workings.

A Simple Rite of Offering at the Home Shrine

This work is intended to introduce students to the Inner experience of the basic Druidic Order of Ritual. It should be administered by an elder ritualist, if possible, with the Elder reading the guidance portions of the text and the student performing the words and deeds of the rite itself. If this is not possible it could be led by one student for another. In either case the Guideshould be certain to experience and project the described visualizations as completely as possible. This helps to create the atmosphere that will draw the student along into the spiritual reality of the Druid's Sacred Grove.

You should have a completed Shrine, and a good, confortable seat placed before it, located so that you can reach all sections of the work area. The Guide will sit close to one side, to recite into your ear. The Guide should be prepared with the full text of the working, while the Ritualist should have only the text of the Shrine Rite of Offering. Materials Needed: Small bell, fire-pot or candle & censer with incense (the Tinteann 'hearth'), cauldron with blessed water the Coire Tobar, or Tobar 'well'), world tree symbol or wand or staff set up as a pillar (Bile 'tree'), images of patron deities, a horn or cup for pouring and drinking, an offering bowl before the Fire if the rite is indoors, offerings (corn meal, silver, olive oil or essential oil,) ale for offering and drinking, and a tool with which to take an omen. The oil might be kept in a vial, from which small offerings are poured, but it is slightly more traditional to use a bowl of oil and a spoon or small ladle to give it to the fire. If one uses incense, then powdered incense spooned on to charcoal gives the same feel. Non-burnable offerings are made into the offering bowl, which is emptied into earth after the rite.

The Working

The Guide and the Ritualist take nine breaths together.

The Guide leads the Nine Breaths Centering, then begins:

So, breathe deep, and feel the flow of the Light and Shadow in your flesh and spirit... you are seated here, at your own Shrine of Druidry... if you have let your eyes close, open them now... breathe, and continue to feel the flow of the Two Powers... let your body relax... settle in your seat... as you gaze upon the symbols and tools of your Shrine remember to hold fast to this relaxation… this detached focus… as you work your rite

You will begin by sounding nine knells or knocks, and making the Opening Prayer:

[1] Give nine knells on a bell, then raise hands to the sky, and say:

I am here to honor the gods. Be with me, Oh Shining Ones, in my working; forgive any errors, and grant me, I pray, your blessing.

So you have begun… breathe deep, feel the flow and shine of the powers, and let your power of vision awaken… let your mind's eye remember the land on which you sit… on which the building that holds your Shrine sits… the land beneath all the human things you know… in that land lives the spirit of the Earth Mother… let your imagination see the Goddess of the land… in whatever form is true for you… as a great woman of strength, wisdom and vast generosity… see her robed and crowned, her form twined with life and changing forms… see her become clear and real in your vision's eye… fill your heart with love for the Earth that sustains you, and open your heart to her love… as you offer to Her…

[2] Offer a pinch of corn meal into the offering bowl, saying:

Earth Mother, I am your child. Mother of all I pray you bless and uphold my rite, as you uphold the whole world. Earth Mother, accept my sacrifice!

Know that the Mother of All underlies all your work… now, in your vision eye, see a triple beam of light shining down upon your from above… turn your palms up to the sky… and let the Three Rays of the Awen shine on your head and hands… this is the Light of Inspiration… the Fire of Wisdom that brings swift, clear power to the Druid's mind… feel its power in you as you honor it, saying:

Place your hands on your heart and open to the light of inspiration, saying:

Power of Inspiration, attend the shrine of my soul. Quicken my tongue that I may work this rite in beauty and in truth.

The Imbas shines down upon you… the Mother of the Land surrounds and supports you… you are about to conjure the Shrine of Druidry, to do as the wise ancients didÖ to make offering to the powers and to come to know the Grove, the Gate and the Blessing… Child of the Earth, is it your will that this be so?…

[3] State the purpose of the rite, saying:

I have come to do as the wise ancients did, to make offering to the powers and to know the Druid's ways. So be it!

Then breathe deep, and feel the flow of the Two Powers in you… and gaze upon your Shrine… upon your Fire and Well and Tree… now take up the silver that you will offer to the Well… see your Coire Tobar filling with the Underworld Power even as the water fills it… you give your offering into the dark waters, as you say…

[4] Offer silver into the cauldron, saying:

In the deeps flow the waters of wisdom. Sacred well, flow within me.

Gaze upon your Tinteann, and make sure that the flame is burning well… take up your offering to the Fire… see the Power of the Heavens fill the common fire in your hearth, shining beneath it's common light… as you make you offering, saying:

[5] Make an offering to the Fire, saying:

I kindle the sacred fire in wisdom, love and power. Sacred fire, burn within me.

Now sprinkle your Bile with water, and see the Dark Power flowing up from beneath.. and cense your Bile with incense or flame, and see the Bright Power flow down in from above… Breathe deep, and see the Fire and Water present in your shrine as they are in your flesh… as you say:

[6] Sprinkle and cense the world-tree, wand or self, saying:

From the deeps to the heights spans the world-tree. Sacred tree, grow within me.

Now the Fire and water are present at the center of your Shrine… as they are present in your heart… breathe deep and fill yourself with the Fire and Water… with these powers you will cleanse the Shrine and yourself… begin to quietly speak the charm of cleansing as you take up the Coire and sprinkle the Shrine and yourself…

[7] See the Deep Power flowing in the whole Shrine washing away ill, repeating:

By the might of the Water and the light of the Fire, this Shrine is made whole and holy

You sprinkle all with the Water and you feel the rinsing of the clean, dark Underworld Power… that washes away the bits and remains of your life's thoughts and deeds… that washes away the half-connected cobwebs of the spirits… leaving you and the Shrine clean… as you replace the Coire and take up the incense…

(Ritualist switches to censing herself and all, continuing the charm.)

As the smoke of the incense drifts, it carries the shining Power of the heavens… that turns every ill to ash… that warms all that it touches, filling all with pure flame… leaving no room for ill… leaving you and your Shrine flowing deep and shining bright… you finish the censing, and return the incense to its place… breathe deep, and spread your hands over your Shrine…

The Center has been blessed, and the Shrine has been cleansed… now fill your Inner Eye with the Middle Realms… the Land on which you rest… the Sky that arcs above you… the Sea that surrounds you… in the Center stand the Fire and Well and Tree… with this vision all around you, speak the charm:

[8] Spread your hands, and encompass the whole shrine in your awareness, saying:

Let the sea not rise, and all ill turn away.
Let the sky not fall and all ill turn away.
Let the land hold firm and all ill turn away.
The Fire, the Well, the Sacred Tree, flow and flame and grow in me!
In Land, Sea, and Sky, below and on high! Thus is the
Sacred Grove claimed and hallowed. So be it!

So, with the Worlds gathered around you… you are seated at your Shrine in the Center of the Worlds… here at the Crossroad of All That Is, you can open a Gate to the Otherworld… first, it is proper to offer to the God of the Gates…

Call up the vision of the Deity who you will ask to aid you in opening the Gate of the Grove… see, if you wish, the Deity's form of flesh… strong and beautiful… you may choose to see the face, eyes shining with secret knowledge… you might see the robes and gems, the tools and weapons of the Keeper of Gates… you may only feel the Deity's presence… an aura of shining, shadowed mist, a power that sees far and opens the roads of seekers… take up your offering, and sacrifice to the God of gates, as you say:

[9] Offer oil or incense to the fire, saying:

I make this offering to the Keeper of the Gates. Gatekeeper, Lord of the Between, Keeper of Roads and Opener of Ways, join your magic with mine to guard and ward the gate of this working. Gatekeeper, accept my sacrifice!

Here, in this place, you have already drawn closer to the Otherworld… already you are surrounded by the Inner Vision of the Worlds… but you can open a deeper gate, here where the Center is strong… a single point, here above your Hallows, that will be for you as the Door of the Otherworld… see the Gate-God turn toward you… hands open… to lend strength to your spell… gaze at your Shrine… and look for a spot that seem to be the Center of the pattern you have woven… breathe deep, and see the power gather there… see a mist form in that spot… put your palms and fingers together, flat… and point your fingers at that spot… as you say:

Now let this sacred center be the boundary of all worlds,
Let the Fire open the Gate
Let the Well open the Gate
Let the Tree hold fast the Way Between.
By the Keeper of Gates, and by my Will and Word, let the Gate be open!

Spread your hands wide… and let your vision eye see the mist part… as though the fabric of your Inner world parted… even the reality of your material air… and see the Gate appear… opening in whatever vision is true and real for you… opening so that you can gaze into it… shining with a shadowed light… a light that is, itself, also the Gate… and so, by this work the Grove is made, and the Gate is open… in this place you can come into the presence of the Spirits… and they into yours…

Now it is proper for you to make your offerings to all the beings of the Worlds… you may not yet have a close knowledge of the Ancestors, the Landspirits and the Deities… but whenever you light the Fire and make the offerings, they will surely turn their faces toward you… open your heart to the Holy Beings, and begin the invocation…

[10] Fill the horn or cup with ale and raise it, saying:

Gods and Dead and mighty Sidhe, Powers of Land and Sky and Sea,
By Fire and Well and sacred Tree, offerings I make to thee!
To those who dwell below, to those who dwell above,
to the tribes of spirits in land, sea or sky.
Hear your true worshipper (your name) as I make due sacrifice.

First you call to the Mighty and Beloved Dead… feel the blood flow in your flesh, and become aware of the Great Chain of Life and Death… the human bodies and spirits, kin of blood and heart, who at bring strength and wisdom from the past… offer to the Ancestors, saying:

Old ones, my ancestors, remember me as I remember you! Ancestors, accept my sacrifice!

Pour a quarter of the ale into the bowl.

Now you call to the Wild and Noble Spirits… feel the breath in your body, the land beneath you, and be aware of the Uncounted Clans of beings who share the world with humankind… who bring wonder and fortune from the worlds' bounty... offer to the Spirits, saying:

Raise the horn, and say:
Spirits of this land, Aid me as I aid you! Spirits accept my sacrifice!
Pour a quarter of the ale into the bowl.

Now you call to the Holy and Shining Deities... the powers of Heaven and the Deep flow in your own spirit... as in the Deities, whose being itself is made of that Fire, that Shadow... the undying Gods and Goddesses of every realm, who bring love and illumination... offer to the Deities, saying:

Raise the horn, and say:

Gods and goddesses of elder days honor me as I honor you! Shining Ones accept my sacrifice!
Pour a quarter of the ale into the bowl and set the horn aside.

As you have made your offerings, so the eyes of the Gods and Spirits are turning toward your Fire, upon the Shrine... the loving faces of the Ancestors... the strange eyes of the Other Kins... the shining gaze of the Goddesses and Gods... open your heart to the Kindreds, as you say:

Mighty, Noble and Shining Ones, be welcome at my Fire! So be it!

So, rest a moment in the presence of the Powers...

If there were other offerings to make—to Gods of the seasons, to especially honor one of the Powers, you would make them now... but it's always proper to work a rite in honor of all the Kindreds together...

Now, as you prepare to make the central sacrifice, open your heart again to all the Powers and Beings of the rite... breathe deep, and let your breath move the power in you, bringing it into your hands... take up your final sacrifice... and hold it in your hands... let the Powers carry all your love and reverence, your awe and you aspiration, into the sacrifice... and give the offering into the Fire, as you give all your worship through the Gate... as you say:

[12] Offer the last of the ale and make an offering of oil to the fire, saying:

Let my voice arise on the flame
Let my voice resound in the well
Oh honored ones, Mighty Dead, Noble Spirits, Shining Gods
Hear me now as I offer up this sacrifice.
Accept my worship and reverence.
Grant me the Druid's Wisdom, and give me your blessing!

Your words, your will and your worship flow up from you, through the Gate, to the Gods and Spirits... for a moment hold the presence of the Powers in your mind, as the smoke of your sacrifice rises to them...

This is the hinge of the rite... until this moment your work has focused on sending your voice and you power outward... you have sought to make yourself heard... now the Powers have received your gifts... have heard your call... and the tide of the rite is turning... turning so that the flow returns from the Gods and Spirits toward you... the focus is now upon you and your Shrine... as the blessing of the Gods comes to you...

First it is proper to seek an omen of the Gods' will and willingness in the rite... open yourself to the flow of power that is beginning to come through the Gate... take up your divining tool and seek an omen, saying:

[13] Cast for a simple omen, with this charm:

(name and nature of the beings one is asking)
I have offered to you.
Now let the true sight be in me, the true speech be mine,
Answer me now, O spirits, what blessing do you offer me, in return for my offerings?

Contemplate the omen… review the meaning of the symbols, and let your mind formulate the message they bring you… the first flow of the Blessing… that now begins to grow stronger… take up your Blessing Cauldron, and pour in the ale, saying:

[14] Refill the horn, saying:

I pour the ale of inspiration, I draw water from the well of wisdom
I fill the cauldron of my spirit, with this drink.
I call upon the Kindreds to give to me as I have given to you, as a gift calls for a gift.

Hold your Blessing Cup up to the gate… and know that into this drink the blessing of the Gods, Dead and Spirits is pouring… in whatever way is true and real for you… a streaming light… a rising shadow… filling your Cauldron… Wisdom, Love and Power that is given to you… yours to accept… see your Cup shining with it, as you say:

Hold your Blessing Cup up to the Gate…

Oh (Patron Powers), hallow these waters! Let this ale be as the Fire of the Gods, as
the Mead of Wisdom
I open my heart to the flow of your blessing, I, your child and worshipper.
Behold the waters of life!

Gaze for a moment into your Cup… see the Blessing that awaits you there… deep in the Waters of Life… the gift of the Holy Worlds… an offering to the Fire and Well within you… now raise your cauldron to your lips and drink… drink deep… and open yourself to the Blessing… feel it in your belly…

Breathe deep, and feel the Two Powers in you… feel the Blessing mingle with them… feeding the Fire… glittering in the Water… filling your loins… your heart… your head… it may be that images arise, as the Blessing fills you… remember this moment, this contact with the power of the Powers… as you say…

In other rites you might bring an intention, a specific goal, and this power would be turned, by your will and your vision, toward that goal… but for now… remember again the vision of the Sacred Grove… the Fire and Well & Tree in the Center… the Underworld beneath… Heavens above… the Land, Sea & Sky spreading out around you… and all the beings in all the worlds… hold this vision, as you affirm the Blessing…

Reverently drink the ale, saying:

The worlds are in me, and I am in the worlds
The spirit in me is the spirit in the worlds
By Fire, Well and Tree; By Gods, Dead and Sidhe;
The blessing flows and shines in me!
Biodh se abhlaidh!

(If you have any remaining work, such as spells in pursuit of the intention, they should be completed at this time.)

So you have received the Blessing of the Powers, and you sit with the Worlds and the Kindreds all around you... now, as you prepare to end your rite, it is proper to give thanks to those who have aided you...

Breathe deep, and let the Blessing shine in you... fill your heart and mind with love for the world and its beings... with gratitude to the Sky, whose air you breathe, to the Land that sustains your life, to the Sea that maintains the balance of all life... be filled with gratitude to the Ancestors, whose lives made yours... to the Landspirits, with whom you share the world... and to the Gods and Goddesses who sustain all the Worlds... breathe deep, spread your hands and let your love and thanks shine out to the boundary of the worlds as you say:

[16] When all is done, give thanks, saying:

> (Patron powers), I give you my thanks!
> Shining Ones, Mighty Dead, Noble Spirits
> I thank you for your aid and blessing.
> Triple Kindreds, Gods, Dead and Landspirits:
> I thank you for upholding my magic.

Now return your attention to the Center... to the gate which stands open... to the Keeper of Gates... give your thanks to the gatekeeper God, saying:

> Lord of the gates, lord of knowledge, I give you my thanks.

So, bring your hands together, fingers pointing toward the Gate, as you say:

[17] Make a closing spiral saying:

> Now let the Fire be flame, the Well be water,
> Let all be as it was before, save for the magic I have made
> Let the Gates be closed!

And see, in whatever way is true and real for you, the gate closing... the Mist draw together over the Center... and as the gate closes, the Vision of the Grove and the Worlds fades... you are seated in your seat, before the Hallows of your Shrine...

Breathe deep, and renew your center... feel the blessing flow in you... this flow of the Two Powers is not something that you ever need to banish... it is the balance within which your life is maintained... but for now, let your awareness of the Fire and water fade... hold fast to every drop and spark that you need... freely release all that you do not...

The rite ends with the Earth Mother, as it began... in every place and at all times, she upholds your life and your work... give her your gratitude, as you say:

[18] Recenter and contemplate the entire working, and end, saying:

> To the Mother I give thanks, for ever upholding my life and my work.

So the rite draws to its close, as you say, at last:

> The fire, the well and the tree
> Flow and flame and grow in me!
> Peace and blessings to all beings,
> The rite is ended!

Part 11

The High Days in Depth

The eight High Days of our Neopagan calendar are the bedrock of ADF's tradition of public Pagan worship and a core element of our spiritual practice. Each of our Groves (ADF's public congregations) is required to offer public ritual on each of these holy feasts. In the same way we ask each of our solitary members to learn the symbolism of the Wheel of the Year, as it is often called, and observe these tides in personal practice.

Introduction to the High Days

What Are The High Days And Where Do They Come From?

The eight High Days are the annual round of Neopagan holy days. They consist of the four 'solar' holidays and the four 'fire festivals' or 'cross-quarter days' which have their best-known expression in Celtic tradition. Together they produce a calendar with sacred occasions spaced evenly every six or seven weeks throughout the year.

Our sacred calendar is not taken directly from any one ancient model. It is a synthesis drawn from several sources. Here we present a short review of the origins of our eight-fold calendar before we discuss how to observe the feasts at home.

European folk tradition retained memories and scraps of pre-Christian tradition in its calendrical customs. Often these customs were preserved in the Christian calendar of saint's days. For instance, the feast of St. John assumed bonfire and agricultural customs retained from Summer Solstice, and, in Germany, St Walburga's Day fell on April 30th. In contrast, many of those days were also associated with 'witchcraft' and all of the church's distorted memories of Pagan worship, feasting and mysteries. When folklorists recorded these seasonal complexes they found them full of the lore of spirits and land-wights, divination and magic.

Early modern scholars observed that ancient monuments such as Stonehenge and Newgrange were aligned to the solstices and equinoxes. They associated these Neolithic sites with the Celtic Druids and, though they were mistaken, the association of Druids with the solar holidays was established in the popular imagination.

In the 18th and 19th century there was a rediscovery of the native literature of Britain and Ireland. The Mabinogion and the tales of Taliesin, the Book of Invasions and the Tain Bo Cuailnge gave a new image of a Celtic and Pagan past. They contain many references to Celtic holy days that had plainly survived in the scraps of folklore.

The earliest British Druidic revival groups made the solstices and equinoxes their ritual occasions. The well-known photos of white-robed Englishmen in long beards at Stonehenge are commonly taken at Summer Solstice. When the first versions of Neopagan Witchcraft were created they began in the same way, but soon added the Fire-feasts to create the eight-fold calendar still in use today.

When ADF was founded in the mid-1980s it chose to simply adopt the nearly universal Neopagan calendar. It was quickly decided to abandon the term 'sabbat', invented by the Church as a slur against the Jews, and the term 'High Days' was adopted in its place. The Wheel of the Year is a construct which never existed in any specific Pagan culture, yet each of the High Days is well-documented as a holy feast in a variety of Indo-European cultures. It is broadly adaptable to our goals, and widely known in the broader Pagan community that we mean to serve. The eight High Days suit both our Indo-European focus and our commitment to Neopaganism.

What Do the High Days Mean?

The lore surrounding each of the eight feasts is deep and complex. You will learn about them in your reading and apply what you learn in your personal path. As an introduction we will examine some of the general spiritual meanings of the High Days.

First, the practice of keeping the Wheel brings an awareness of the land in which you dwell. The seasonal nature of the feasts creates a personal feel for the life and flow of the land. We find a core spiritual value in the attunement of our minds and lives to the turn and return of the annual cycle of sun and earth.

We see the simple, public purpose of our round of seasonal worship to be the creation and maintenance of a flow of blessing from the Gods and Spirits to ourselves, our homes and our folk, and even to all the world. Pagan religion accepts the role of human ritual in maintaining the relationship between the divine and the world of common life. Our offerings, our fires, our songs help to bring us the help from the gods that we need in our lives. Our Gods love and respect us as we do them, and they use their power to aid us. As Pagans have ever done, we seek health, wealth and wisdom in our lives and wisdom, love and power in our souls.

In Indo-European cultures the annual round of feasts and sacrifices included many of the major deities and lesser spirits of the local Pagan religion. When we observe each of the feasts throughout the year we, too, work with a broad selection of the Gods and Spirits of our chosen cultures. The powers of love and death, hearth and forest, commerce and war, of sowing and reaping, and the hunt may all be invited into our lives. A polytheistic system seeks the depth and detail of the divine power in the many beings of the spiritual world, and working a year of the Wheel leads us to invoke each of these powers in turn. This work creates a balance of the Powers in the life of the worshipper. As we approach the Gods in worship, we awaken in ourselves their own images and presences, and glimpse some spark of the divine fire. Through the keeping of the Wheel we bring the natural balance and beauty of the seasons, and the power of the Gods, into our own lives. When we observe the High Days, even in a simple way, we open our own souls to a balanced progression of the Divine Powers.

The spiritual work of the High Days is performed on a scale of years, at the pace of sun and earth, yet there are many fine blessings for those working their first year to be gained from each day in turn. Each completed observation of a full turning of the Year places your own soul at the center of a grand mandala of all the powers of the sacred world. As with all of our rituals in this Dedicant's path, the best way to begin is simply to begin—choose a few simple things, and turn your mind toward the land and the gods.

Understanding the Practice of the High Days

Looking At the Lore

As you approach your first High Day it is good to spend a bit of preparation time reviewing the lore and customs of the feast. You may decide simply to adopt one of the rituals we provide in our support materials. These rites cannot themselves provide you with real depth of understanding of the complex meanings of each of the holy days. As in every part of our work you will need to read and study to reach a working understanding of the High Days.

Ethnic Options

One of the first choices you will need to make is within which Indo-Europeans (IE) culture you will work your High Day. ADF is neither attempting to recreate any specific ancient culture, nor to create a generic modern Paganism. Rather we mean to study the specific traditions of ancient peoples and to create modern systems based on them. As part of our first century of work we have chosen to attempt to work our rites within only one ancient culture at a time. While this rule is frequently bent, we encourage you to choose just one cultural model in which to work any specific High Day rite. You may come to ADF with a clear notion of which ancient culture excites and inspires you, or you may feel a need to experiment. It is common for new students to work one High Day in one culture and the next in another, but we discourage you from mixing elements from various cultures in any single rite.

We are still in our early stages of understanding what ancient Pagan religions were really like, and what those ways can mean to us today. ADF has always been defined by a few 'game rules' of our experiments—not dogmas, but self-identifying guidelines. One of those is our choice to work our rites in one specific culture at a time.

Of course ADF makes another 'game rule' of limiting our choices to the Indo-European peoples. If you wish to work in Chinese or Incan systems we may be interested in the results, but it won't be an ADF ritual. To choose which culture to work in for your first efforts you can simply select one that interests you. You may already be drawn to the Celtic, Hellenic, Slavic or some other culture or ways. You may have a connection through ethnic heritage, or simply by fascination with a body of mythology. ADF places no importance on ethnic, genetic or 'blood' background—feel free to choose from the long list of Indo-European cultures. You may be drawn to some part of your family heritage or to another culture entirely. In your early efforts you need not overthink your choices. Simply pick a pantheon that interests you, and begin.

The Land & the Seasons

Your local climate and landscape should influence how you approach the High Days. Druidry is always local religion, grounded in the soil we walk on, not in cosmic principles that transcend landscape. The land, water, weather, plants and beasts of your environment will be the presence of the divine in your High Day experience.

As each High Day draws near be sure to observe the actual changes in the material world around you. Our High Days are generally based on cultures that lived in somewhat northerly places. Even in the tropics the stars wheel with the seasons, and winds and waters vary their patterns. Learn about your local growing seasons, what crops and resources are harvested in what times and how the major native animals live through their year.

Gods and Spirits

As you prepare for a High Day you will need to decide which of the Gods and Spirits you will address. You should make an effort to examine the myths and customs of the Pagan culture you prefer to find hints of which Gods are proper to the Day. Folklore tends to disguise the Old Gods behind medieval saints and wonder-tales and these tales are full of hints and snippets that resonate with older lore.

We have formal calendars preserved from some IE Paganisms that list Gods proper to each season. The Roman and Hellenic calendars, for instance, are very detailed, but do not fit with great ease into our eight-fold year. In many other cultures you must choose for yourself what Gods you will worship based on your reading and intuition.

Some Pagans prefer to choose a God and a Goddess for each feast, others do not concern themselves with gender balance in that way. Some High Days in some cultures are plainly devoted primarily to a single deity. In other cases the lore may focus on one of the other Kindreds—on the Ancestors or the beings of the Land. We offer some simple support materials but in the end you must choose for yourself which of the Gods and Spirits you will honor.

Customs and Lore

Each of the seasonal holy days is observed with a variety of customs. Songs, dances, fires, purifications, handicrafts and meals along with nearly every other sort of human activity are employed by various cultures for the feasts. You will choose just a very few customs to observe for your first High Days.

Once again the easiest way to focus your choices is to draw upon a single Pagan culture. Use your sources—books and internet articles—to locate two or three customs that you can accomplish on a small scale. You might choose to dye eggs for Spring Equinox, along with blessing seed or ground for your year's garden. You might choose a warrior's hike for Lughnassadh along with baking a loaf for offering.

Seasonal customs can be divided into offerings and blessings. It is always proper to give offerings to the Gods and Spirits, whether food for the Dead at the November Feast or flowers for the Landwights at the Summer Feast. We always look for their blessings in turn, whether the purifying fire of May or the peace and feasting of Winter. As you review your sources you might look for one custom to use for offering, and one for blessing.

Working the High Days

Your First High Days

In our Groves we often make a festive liturgical occasion of a High Day. Robes, tools, symbols and songs come together in well-worked group ritual. As a student of Druidry you have the chance to learn to work fully developed solitary Druidic sacrifice. You will create your own sacred tools and hallows, pour offerings and sing chants. In many ways the work of creating your own Druidry is the work of becoming your own priest.

Even for a brand-new student, keeping the seasonal feasts is one of the simple pleasures of the Pagan way. From the very first days of your Pagan journey, even when you do not yet feel ready to work full ritual, you can find easy ways to bring the power of the year's cycle into your life. Homely customs based in food and fire, land and family, are easily done by beginners.

As you approach your first High Day you can choose from several levels of complexity. At the simplest you can add a simple seasonal invocation to your daily or weekly practice, perhaps along with a seasonal household handicraft. If you have introduced yourself to our full Druidic ritual structure (perhaps through the Self-Blessing ritual) you can choose to work a simple seasonal rite at your hearth or home shrine. As you become comfortable with our ritual forms you may wish to set up a full Nemeton (ritual space) in a room or outdoors, and work a full rite with family or friends.

Preparing For a High Day

No matter which level of work you begin with, you will need to prepare for the day in advance. You should spend some time in study, looking at what reliable sources have to say about the symbolism and customs surrounding the season and its feast. Note the phase of the moon and the nature and condition of the soil, plants, water and beasts. Choose very specifically which ceremony, customs, charms or prayers you will use. Make good copies of the texts whether or not you plan to read from them during the actual work. Be sure your ritual tools are ready, and make or obtain any unusual props or symbols called for by the ritual before the day.

On the day before the High Day make certain that you have each and every item that you mean to use. Have your text ready, and read it frequently to become familiar with it. Prepare the indoor or outdoor space you mean to use. If possible spend the evening before in quiet reading, meditation and rest.

A Simple High Day

If you don't feel ready and able to work a full ritual for your first High day you can still be open to the season's blessings. Customs based in home and hearth can be combined with simple bits of ceremony. The key is to be mindful of the season and the living earth, and diligent in your reading and study of the seasonal lore.

When you rise on the High day you should bathe and then work some simple centering or devotion. If you have a regular morning practice then you should do that. Otherwise a rite from this guide, such as the Simple Devotion or even the First Rite should be performed. If you wish you can add some simple statement of intent for the High Day, such as:

Hear me all Kindreds; today I will keep the feast of (Samhain). Let the wisdom of the land be clear to me, the memory of the Old Ways grow strong in me and the blessings of the Powers flow and shine in me on this feast of (the Honored Dead).

During the day you can keep whatever customs you have chosen. Perhaps you can walk in a patch of woods and spend a while reading poetry or story from the culture in which you're working. At your evening meal you might set aside a portion of food for the spirits, with such words as you like.

Once you have established a shrine in your own home you can celebrate each High Day by decorating it for the season. Flowers, greenery and symbolic objects can be combined artfully to bring the feel of the High Day to your home altar. This is a simple but gracious expression of the season that can be extended to your whole house, if you wish.

Some people choose to make the evening meal the most ritualized moment of an informal High Day. It can be a time, especially with family or a small group, for lighting candles, passing cups and recitation of prayers. Another good time for the performance of customs is sunset. If you can be outdoors in the gloaming of twilight, especially if alone, it can be a powerful moment for a small seasonal charm or invocation. We give a small selection of such charms in this guide, and our internet resources offer a wealth of material.

Conclusion

The Wheel of the Year is one of the core mysteries of Our Druidry. The eight High Days combine the realities of the local land with all the deepest mythic patterns of the Old Ways. As you work a few years of the Wheel you will begin to feel the spiritual rhythm of the cycles, and your understanding of the High Days will continue to grow throughout your life.

Part 12

Personalizing Your Paganism

When you have learned the order of ritual and established your ritual tools, you are prepared to enter, or to deepen, a personal relationship with the gods, goddesses, ancestors and spirits. The work of building a personal Paganism leads directly to this contact with the otherworld powers, and it is through these powers–by joining our own power with that of the Gods and Spirits–that further spiritual work is possible. So we encourage students to build a personal, or perhaps family, religion of the hearth.

Ancient Paganism was decentralized. While whole clans might gather for High Day rites, there were no weekly communal gatherings at places of worship - no 'churches'. Instead, Paganisms were based at the hearths of clans and families. Each garth, each steading, would have it's household Gods, the Deities of the professions practiced by its folk, it's goddesses of bounty and protection. As you move beyond the basic Druidic commitments of your First Oath, we encourage you to make your hearth, your Home Shrine, into a temple not only of Our Druidry, but of your own Paganism.

Many of those who choose to work as solitary Pagans seek the skills to function as their own priests. It is in this phase of the work that one moves from worshipping the Gods and Spirits on an occasional basis to keeping a personal relationship with them. This is the basis of personal priesthood, in which one's own hearth becomes the temple of one's own Gods and Allies.

The Nature of The Gods & Spirits

One of the goals of ADF's work is to rebuild religions that are truly polytheistic. We encourage you, perhaps as a thought experiment, to view the gods as the gods–as independent, self-existent beings with whom we share the worlds. We try not to view them as 'archetypes' in the 'collective unconscious' or as 'aspects of ourselves'. We do not view them as aspects of a great Goddess and Great God, nor as faces of any single Divine Person. This approach, we feel, speaks to the wonder of diversity in both the natural and divine worlds–the glory of the many Gods and Goddesses, the Company of the Halls of Wonder. Of course none of this 'doctrine' is required for the work. We present it here only as a core game-rule around which our systems have been developed, and by which they operate.

So we work in a vast company of the Shining Gods, the Mighty Dead, the Noble Spirits. While this vision is delightful and inspiring, it may also seem rather distant, and even intimidating. How can a common mortal approach these powers in any way more personal than public sacrifice? Tradition provides a simple, powerful answer in the practice of Hearth Paganism–the construction of a personal pantheon, gathered from the 'menu' of the spirits. You will make a personal alliance with specific Gods or Goddesses, with beings of the Dead and the Landspirits. Thus you gain teachers, protectors, and supporters, who can help you in your relationships with the other deities and spirits, and be there for you in the trials and joys of your life.

Personal relationship with the Powers is one of the foundations of a strong personal Paganism. The Powers are to the worshipper as a teacher to a student, as a maze to the curious, as a haven to the harried, and as a beloved godparent to a child. The presence of divine wisdom, love and power is brought directly into your home, shining and flowing from your home shrine. When trouble comes, the Hearth Gods are strength and comfort, and when life is good, they are blessing and wisdom.

By entering into relationship with the Powers you will learn to be assured of the care and support of mighty beings, who have a breadth and depth of understanding far greater than your own, and magic that can shape reality. So when you have begun your hearth worship, when the Hearth Gods have begun to speak to you in vision and omen, you can begin to ask boons and seek personal empowerment.

This may be the first kind of practical magic that you undertake. To go to the shrine and make an appeal to mighty allies, and see that boon granted, teaches the reality of the power of the Gods as little else can. Of course, you should be moderate and wise in your requests, and not view the Gods as a sort of 'wishing bottle.' If you ask the Powers first to grant you the blessings of wisdom and compassion and vigor, you may not often have to ask for their special intervention in your life.

When you have chosen, or been chosen by, your Hearth Gods and allies, you will have completed these first steps of our magic. You will have learned a great deal about yourself and your soul, and gained your first teacher and friend in the spirit-world.

Seeking the Hearth Gods

In this simple instruction, we can offer only a few exercises to help you in the process of making the alliance with the Gods. For some, the process will be simple: the study of lore and the practice of rites, the course of your life, may make it simply obvious. For others, the work will take longer and require more effort.

There are some who say that you do not choose an ally, but rather are chosen by a deity, or ancestor, or landspirit as their own. This may well be so. The power of a god is such that even as you seek a patron the deity may be weaving the fate that brings you to them. So it is fine to diligently pursue the discovery of your patrons and allies, even as you understand that you will succeed only when a god or spirit claims you as his own.

We offer a few hints:

Study and Contemplation: The first step in seeking allies is to read, study and truly integrate the lore of a Pagan culture. You should choose one or two cultures in which to immerse yourself. If you haven't made the choice of a key culture, that is your first step, though sometimes the call of the patron leads you to the culture, rather than the other way around. But the work of taking the tales, symbols and meanings of Pagan lore into yourself will provide the raw material for the patron's call.

We encourage you to seek scholastically sound sources. You should also seek to understand the music and life of the cultures. Listen to recordings, eat the traditional foods, perhaps seek out the modern remnants of the culture in your community. While scholarly sources are key to understanding, well-researched fictions, songs and poems can shed the light of poetic inspiration on the dry facts of scholarship, and help you to integrate a feeling for the Old Ways.

This study should provide inspirations for contemplation and meditation. These can be added to one's daily or weekly Shrine work, though we recommend that you make every effort to do some of this meditation out of doors. Perhaps your nature attunement work will have found several places in your community where you can be fairly certain of being undisturbed. Relax, and let the images and ideas of your study flow through your mind. You may find yourself drawn to one or more of the deities from the tales, you may see animal or plant omens of the influence of a deity in the natural forms around you. Let your mind flow in peaceful entrancement, listen and observe.

Symbol Sorting: You may find a clue to your soul's leanings by examining your reactions to potent symbols. You might start with the tarot, perhaps one of the new, more Celtic or Norse or Hellenic decks, using only the major trumps. Or you might choose one of the non-tarot oracle decks, and possibly do this exercise with several different systems. For this exercise, you should choose a system with actual pictures, rather than abstract forms like the Norse runes. You might use a familiar set of images, or choose one you've never seen before and use your first exposure to it to gauge your reactions.

Take your set of symbols and look through them. As you look at each image, make a simple judgement. Do you like the image? Does it feel strong? Friendly? Attractive? Even if you don't like it, does it move or excite you? Begin by sorting the symbols into, perhaps, three piles - not very interesting, interesting, and very interesting. Set aside the uninteresting cards and again sort the interesting ones, until you reach just a few - perhaps one or two. The short list of symbols at which you arrive can provide clues as to which of the deities may be right for you.

This is not divination. Don't assume that this process is a sure way of choosing a deity. Try to work through a few different symbol systems, then take the resulting symbols and make them the object of your meditations. One direct and practical application of this method is to place the images that move you on your home shrine. Thus, even if one does not yet know the names of the deities one seeks, one can begin to approach them through those symbols.

Seeking in Vision: The work of seeking the patron is one of your first opportunities to practice the skills of vision–of approaching the otherworld through will and imagination. The trance-scripts that follow this article will provide basic patterns for altering your awareness and entering trance. While we ask you to try the scripts as written, you are of course encouraged to adapt them to your own needs and ideas.

To use a script of this sort, first read it through thoroughly and become familiar with the sequence of images. You may wish to tape the whole script. If so, be certain to read it very slowly, leaving plenty of silence in places that seem to need it. The most skilled approach is to simply to remember the phases of the trance and let the images lead you where they may.

This information might have been included in the Meditation portion of our training. However, vision-work requires a basic skill in meditation and visualization, The work of establishing the shrine and learning the rites, should have sharpened your abilities, and so we have included this next stage of trance and vision work in this section. The first script is a simple way to approach the otherworld, a general gate vision, that can get you started. The second trance has been helpful to students, and we offer it for the time when you feel like the patron may be drawing near.

Choices and Expectations

The Allies can make themselves clear to you in many ways, or can lead you with the subtlest of hints. We can only suggest that you will, in the end, simply know who they are, either through clear vision, through omen or through certainty of mind. It will then be proper to make a rite of patronage, or to install the Allies as images or symbols in your Hearth Shrine, and take up the personal work and worship of that god or goddess, and the honoring of the spirits. You will learn to listen for their voice, to draw on their strength to speak to them in your heart. In turn you will offer them worship and respect, offerings of food and incense and praise.

It is said that, in the end, the Deities choose us as their people, and, even as we actively seek alliance with the Ancestors and the Spirits, they make the choice to aid us. But there is also no harm in beginning to honor a deity one feels certain about, and then looking for confirmation. The gods are seldom jealous about such things, and just beginning the work can precipitate the success you seek.

So try to suspend your expectations about what sort of spirits will answer your call. Don't assume that your work or interests or life makes you an automatic object of any god's patronage. Surprises are common in these matters, though sometimes everything works out just as properly and orderly as one would like.

The work of building your hearth religion is a means by which the powers can educate and empower their worshippers, drawing us into the work of wisdom. Your first allies will be important to you for your whole life, but it is true that patrons and spiritual co-workers do change sometimes. Sometimes these are simply additions to one's personal work, sometimes one Power steps aside in favor of another. In the many realms and worlds, among the many gods, goddesses and spirits, there is room for a lifetime's growth, and more.

Kindred Attunement Work

With a little exploring, find a place in your area that seems to speak to you of one of the Kindreds. Take to the place a simple vessel for water, and a fire-bowl. That can be as simple as a bowl with three candles, or perhaps a bit of fire-starter or fatwood in an iron cauldron. Take also some simple offerings for the Spirits.

Find a spot where you can comfortably sit to meditate. Sprinkle the water deisil around the space, then light the fire bowl. Lift the fire to the sky, then set it on the earth, saying:

The Fire, the Well, the Sacred Tree
Flow and flame and grow in me.
By Land Sea and Sky
Below and on high
I come to this place to greet the spirits.

Then sit, with the fire and water before you, and draw the Two Powers into yourself. Then take up your offering, and, if you like, imagine the form and presence of whatever kindred you are seeking. Recite aloud a simple invocation, such as:

Ancestors: O Mighty Ones, my ancestors, my kindred, I, your worshipper, honor you. You whose life and death creates my life, whose wisdom upholds my wisdom, I come to you in peace. Mighty Dead, I honor your presence, offering my love and worship, and this (sacrifice). Be with me in my heart and in my work, and accept this gift in token of our kinship. Ancestors, I pray you, accept my sacrifice.

Nobles: Oh Noble Ones, my allies, with whom I share the worlds, I honor you. Spirits of stone and stream, red kins and green kins, peoples of the Otherworld, I come to you in peace. Noble Spirits, I honor your presence, offering my love and worship, and this (sacrifice). Be with me in my heart and in my work, and accept this gift in token of our friendship. Noble Ones, I pray you, accept my sacrifice.

Deities: Oh Shining Ones, my Elders, Goddesses and Gods, wisest and mightiest, I honor you.. You who sustain the worlds, first Children of the Mother, Tribe of the Goddess, I come to you in peace. Shining Deities, I honor your presence, offering my love and worship, and this (sacrifice). Be with me in my heart and in my work, and accept this gift in token of my worship. Shining Ones, accept my sacrifice.

Give the offering to the land in whatever way, and then practice the Earth Attunement meditation. Allow all ideas of the form of the Spirits to flow away into the silence, and bask in direct experience of the land. Finish by saying:

The Fire, the Well, the Sacred Tree
Flow and flame and grow in me
I give thanks to all beings who have witnessed or aided in this work,
And declare it ended.
So be it!

A Trance to Discover Hearth Gods

Following some work at discovering hints and symbols of your patron deities, choose one or two symbols to focus on for meditation. They might be runes, animal or natural signs, or any symbol that has become connected with the quest.

* Perform a simple rite of offering to all the spirits, asking to be shown the way to the patrons. Take up your posture for meditation, with the symbols before you. Begin basic meditation, and contemplate the symbols without thought. Assure yourself that you will effortlessly remember the symbols in trance.

* Work the Passing the Mist exercise, and step forth in the vision locale of your Inner Nemeton. After you have oriented yourself, turn to the West, and see there a path leading toward a meadow.

* Walking a short path through woods you arrive at a great rolling meadow. In the distance the green and black forest rolls away to the horizon. You move slowly and gently over the plain, on the soft grass and herbs. You turn toward where the forest looms in the distance and begin to walk toward that green shadow.

* As you walk, take note of your surroundings. Is the sky clear? Overcast? Stormy? Is the meadow green and level, hilly, thorny and rough, or desert? Whatever the condition of the plain, you will see at least a few flowers among the plants. You reach out and pluck three blossoms and carry them with you.

* You walk toward the forest's edge. After a while you see before you two great pillars of wood, decorated with every holy sign, each upon a mound, with the path opening between them. Along the path toward the greenwood you see two lines of symbol-carved pillars, stretching to the wood's edge. You know that this is the road for you to follow, the wide, flat path between the signs.

- You venture down the avenue of pillars, and as you near the edge of the forest you see that the avenue ends at a small temple, a simple, square building, brightly painted, with a porch on which is a raised fire altar of stone. The door of the little temple is closed and on each side of the doors is an empty niche, made as if to hold and image.

- Your seeking to know and honor your patron deities has brought you to here, clearly the place appointed. So you reverently approach the altar and place your three blossoms there in offering. Open your heart to the patrons, whether or not you know their names, and invoke them by your love and devotion. As you open your heart a spark of flame descends from above and blooms into fire in the altar. Your blossoms flame, but wondrously are not consumed. As the flowers flame with the blessing of the patrons, the doors of the temple swing quietly inward. In that doorway is darkness and swirling, like grey winter-night mist. You feel a presence, a power waiting in the shrine. Though it is an awe-inspiring feeling, you know that it stands aside for you to enter, and you step into the temple. Lining the walls of the room, you see images of dozens of deities, gods and goddesses, each made to fit the niches on the porch of the temple.

- Now you must choose. If you open your heart, you may know which images you will honor. Take them out to the porch of the temple and place them in their niches. Return to stand before the fire and bathe in the light of the flame contemplating the images and calling out to the spirits of the deities.

- It may be that no deity calls to you at this time. If that is the case, simply return to the fire of devotion in front of the shrine.

- Meditate for a time, open to the voice of the patrons.

When you have finished, you may wish to make a request to the deities, then turn and walk back down the avenue of pillars. Know that the fire of devotion will burn on that altar as long as you truly honor these deities, or await your patrons, in your heart. As you walk, you see the light of your own Sacred Fire and you move across the landscape toward it. As you go the silver mist encloses you and you find yourself once again standing in your own Inner Temple. You return to your physical form, coming fully into your body, to common time and place, fully and firmly as you open you eyes and return to common awareness.

Part 13

The Dedicant's Oath

The Dedicant's Oath

Our magic is often focused on the community, on the human family's relationship with the gods, goddesses and spirits. It can also be a way of spiritual growth, of initiation into mystery. It can provide structure for a pattern of growth, with clear markers along the way. When your work has reached a certain level it is proper to take a formal oath of dedication to Pagan Druidry.

This oath is a proclamation to the inner self that you are on the path. It builds a deeper connection between your spirit, the hallows of your shrine, and the cosmic order. It works to open a gate of the spirits in your heart, and sends a call to those who might aid your work.

This oath is the crown of the first stage of our Druidic work. It says to others along the way that you have gained an understanding of our core symbols and ritual patterns. It says that your work is recognized by fellow Pagans and that you have taken a significant step into a like-minded spiritual family.

When should you take the oath?

It is proper to take the dedicant's oath when you are certain that you want to walk in the Pagan way; when you want to know nature and the Earth as sources of deep spiritual wisdom. It is taken when you know that you are drawn to the religions and magics of pre-Christian Europe; when the old gods and goddesses are calling to your soul. It is time for the oath when: you have kept the holy days for at least a full year; you have gained a grounding in the old lore from true sources; you may feel sure you know which of the Pagan pantheons you will choose as your own; you have learned the basics of meditation, trance and vision; you have established your home shrine; you have done home offerings and understand the order of ritual. When all this is done, or at least well begun, it is the time to take the dedicant's oath.

Preparing the Rite

For most people, the oath rite will be a solitary working, although a couple or family might choose to perform it together. If a small group or new grove has been pursuing the dedicant's work together they might also take the oath together. If a student or group has worked with a Senior Druid or initiate in their training they might ask that teacher to be present. But the oath can always be done alone.

It's probably best if the rite can be done out of doors, but you may prefer to perform it at your own shrine. If you can go outdoors, you will need to find a place where you will not be disturbed. Secluded spots on shorelines or by water, on a hilltop, even a gorge or cave, can be evocative and powerful. You will need to pack up your shrine hallows so that you can recreate it under the sky and upon the Earth. If possible you should create the sacred center directly upon the ground. While in many outdoor areas you will need to keep the fire in a vessel, it is better if you can build a fire on the Earth. You may be able to make a raised fire altar by cutting squares of sod from the four corners of your working area and bringing them to the center. You will also need a cauldron or vessel to represent the well, perhaps filled with water from the immediate area. If possible you might dig a deep, narrow hole into which you can place offerings. Ideally, all of this would be set up at the root of a great oak tree.

But none of that may be practical. Even if you can work outdoors you may wish to use your regular hallows, which is fine. Even if you must tuck them into a corner of your backyard, it may be preferably to working indoors. It is for you to decide.

If possible, choose a night for your rite that will coincide with the waxing moon or full moon, when the air is calm and the sky mostly clear. You should plan the rite so that you can begin just before sunset, work the rite through dusk and end in full darkness.

You will need all of the offerings for a full rite. In addition, you will need a special item, a piece of jewelry or other decoration meant to symbolize your commitment to Druidic Paganism. You may want to suit the symbol to your cultural choice: those following a Celtic path might choose a torc, Norse devotees a Thor's Hammer, etc. For general purposes you might choose any threefold symbol, or our Druid sigil.

This sign will stand as a reminder of your dedication to your spiritual path. It will be consecrated to the powers of the cosmos, to the gods, goddesses and spirits, and to your own spirit. It symbolizes the knot that binds you to the world order. This symbol is your first badge of honor on our Druid way.

For many students, this will be the most focused and intense work that you have yet undertaken. We hope you will approach this step with care, with sincere aspiration, and with joy.

A Dedicant's Oath Rite

The following rite utilizes skills that you have learned earlier in the program (see page 22.) As taking an oath is very personal, you should tailor this rite to fit your own tastes and needs. Below, you will find several suggested alternatives, marked with asterisks. Choose the one that best suits you, or insert your own wording.

[1] Beginning
    Musical signal
    Circle the hallows three times

[2] Opening prayers
    Earth Mother
    Inspiration
    Outdwellers and purification

[3] Meditation and attunement

[4] Statement of purpose

I come into the sacred grove of the elder ways, toward the sacred center, to the meeting place of the worlds. I, (your name), approach the gods in pride and wonder, as a seeker of blessing, bringing offerings in honor of all of the kins of spirits. I come to the well and kindle fire to make an oath of dedication to the path of the old wisdom, the eternal way.

I come to give my worship to the gods and goddesses, to the beloved and wise dead, and to all the Kindreds and spirits with whom I share the worlds. Especially I bring offerings to (name deity and attributes). I ask them to bear witness to my oath, and guide and ward my way.

As the ancient wise did before me, so I seek to do now. Let every holy power hear me, and look kindly on me as I make my oath.

[5] Well

[6] Fire

[7] Tree

[8] Land, sea and sky

[9] Opening the gate

[10] Triad offerings

Ancestors

A child of the earth calls out to the mighty dead. Hear me, I pray, O ancestors, my kindred.

(Pour some ale on the Earth, in the shaft or in the offering bowl)

I offer to you, mighty ones. To the ancient tribes of this place, you whose bones lie in this land; to my own blood-kin and heart-kin; to the elder wise, druids and warriors and farmers of ancient days, to you I give welcome at my sacred fire.

(Pour ale)

I offer to you, O sustainers of life. I ask you to hear my voice and witness my oath. I pray you to guide my ways as I walk the path of Pagan wisdom, the Druid's way. Mighty dead, accept my offering:

(pour ale)

Spirits

A child of the earth calls out to the tribes of spirits. Hear me, I pray, O companions, my allies.

(Sprinkle some herbs or stones at the tree's base)

I offer to you, noble ones. To the Kindreds of stone and stream; to those of leaf and root and shoot, to those of fur and feather and scale. To all, I give welcome at my sacred fire.

(Make offerings)

I offer to you, wild ones, lovely ones. I ask you to hear my voice and witness my oath. I pray that you will open my way as I walk the way of the earth in reverence, the druid's way. Spirit clans, accept my offering.

(Make offerings)

Deities

A child of the Earth calls out to the shining ones. Hear me, I pray, gods and goddesses of old time.

(Make offering of oil or incense to the fire)

I offer to you, shining ones. To all the first children of the Mother, the wisest and mightiest; to all the deities of this land, known or unknown; to those mighty ones who watch over my own soul, to you I give welcome at my sacred fire.

(Make offering)

I offer to you, eldest and brightest. I ask you to hear my voice and witness my oath. I pray you empower my ways as I walk the path of divine magic, the Druid's way. Shining deities, accept my offering.

Druid chants:

*Gods and dead and spirits all
Hear my offering, hear my call
By fire and well and sacred tree
From land and sky, and from the sea
Now come, I pray you, to the grove
and bring your wisdom, strength and love.*

Pause to meditate for a while on the presence of the host of spirits you have called. Speak in your heart to whichever of them may present themselves to you, and listen for their voices.

[11] Key offerings

As you approach this work you may find yourself in one of two positions. First, you may have already made a clear connection with one or more deities, and have a preference for that worship. You may feel that there are gods or non-gods that you would want to give special honor to in this rite. Or, you may still be seeking and awaiting these special personal contacts, even though you feel sure of your dedication. Your feelings about this will influence how you approach the key offerings.

If you don't have a clear constellation of powers you wish to invoke, then the triad invocations will be your main invocations. You will gather the host of spirits and make your oath to them. If there are specific powers you wish to invite, then you will have prepared invocations for each, or perhaps a single invocation that addresses your personal list. You will also have prepared personal offerings for each. Envision the presence of your powers, recite the invocation, and give them the offerings.

The Oath Offerings

The last and greatest offering is made as you actually pronounce the oath. The giving of the oath is itself an offering or sacrifice. It is the offering of a link between your own life and the gods and spirits, a kind of relationship not unlike taking a lover or a blood-brother. You are proposing to enter into the ancient bargain, the first simple agreement that binds the common world of life to the undying other. Choose the words of your oath with care. It is not our place or our intention to set a specific set of words to this first oath. It must come out of your own skill, your own path. But we do offer some ideas to consider making part of your oath, and one or two possible versions.

- Expression of your commitment to the Pagan ways, to the old religion of Europe or your people of choice.

- Expression of honor for the spirits. This can be expressed as the three kins. Special reference should be made to any personal allies.

- Expression of possible goals: health, wealth and wisdom, enlightenment, etc.

[12] The Oath Sacrifice

You will have a special offering prepared for this final giving of the oath. The oath is, itself, the prayer of sacrifice for this rite. Recite it with a whole heart and give your offering.

Possible text for the oath:

A child of Earth comes to the sacred grove to make an oath to the powers of the worlds. I come by the road of seeking, through the door of new learning, to the fire of inspiration, to the well of wisdom, to the gates between the worlds. Hear me, O powers, as I offer up these sacrifices. I give you these gifts, I give you my oath as an offering in your honor. O mighty, noble and shining ones, hear me, I pray.

I am [Your Name] of the family of [Family or Clan], and it is my will to walk the Pagan way. So I swear by the gods and by the dead and by all the spirits. I swear to live by the virtues given by tradition, to strive to live well and do good.

I swear to keep the feasts and observances of the Druid way, keeping the wheel of the year. I swear to seek the truth of the elder ways, to learn the lore and meaning of our ancestors' wisdom. These things I swear by the well that flows in me, by the fire that shines in me, by the tree that roots and crowns my soul.

Before all the powers, and especially before my god(s) [Name of God(s)], I swear it. May the three worlds rise against me if I am forsworn. So be it!

Now let my voice arise on the fire, let my voice resound in the well, let my words pass the boundary to the spirits. Mighty, noble and shining ones, accept my sacrifice and my oath!

[13] The Omen

The omen is taken, asking what blessing the powers offer the dedicant in return for her offering. If an elder is witnessing the rite the elder might do this for the dedicant, but it is well if the dedicant has the skill to do so herself.

[14] A Charm for Blessing the Dedicant's Cup

In order to work this blessing you will need three charm-items. The first is a globe of jet or onyx, no larger than a marble. The second is a small, perfect quartz point, no more than an inch long. The third is a bit of stone half of one color and half of another, perhaps red and green. The first is the stone of the underworld, the second the stone of the heavens and the third of the place between and the manifest world.

These stones should be set on the shrine for three days before the rite, then washed and rinsed well. The drink used in the blessing cup should be that which is most pleasing to your own palate: Guinness, good wine, ice tea, root beer or whatever. Take up the blessing cup in your left hand and recite this charm of blessing, dropping in the stones when called for.

Ancient and mighty ones, I have honored you. Now I pray you honor me in turn, for a gift calls for a gift. I thirst for the waters of wisdom, of bounty and rebirth, from the bosom of the Earth Mother. I open my heart to the blessing of the great ones, and pray you hallow these waters.

(Drop the black sphere into the cup.)

May the dark waters of the underworld rise in this cup of blessing. As I drink, may I know the depths of the world's chaos, the all-potential in which I am rooted. May the Mother of all know me, and grant me wisdom, love and power.

(Drop the crystal point into the cup)

May the shining light of the heavens blaze in this cup of blessing. As I drink it, may I know the heights of the world's order, the seed of life that quickens the spirit. May the fire father know me, and grant me wisdom, love and power.

(Drop the two-colored stone into the cup)

In this cup of blessing the two powers meet. Let it be as a boundary place, and let magic be its substance. As I drink let the way Between be open in my heart. May the keeper of gates know me, and grant me wisdom, love and power.

Now I pray to you, O spirits, hallow these waters, and I will rejoice in your gift. Bless my spirit and my life with health, bounty and wisdom as I drink the sacred waters. Behold the waters of life!

[15] The Blessing

Slowly and contemplatively, drink most of the blessing cup. As you sip renew your center, and feel yourself drinking in the power of the gods and spirits. Take up your dedication token and anoint it with the waters of life. Say:

By the might of the waters and the light of the fire, by the three Kindreds in the three worlds do I bless this token. May it serve always to remind me of my oath as I wear it near my flesh. Let the blessing of the powers shine and flow in it, turning aside ill and kindling wisdom, love and power in my spirit. So be it!

Put on the token. If you wish, this is the time to perform an incantation of personal power, a lorica or power song that can come either from your feeling of the moment or from tradition.

When all this is done, sit before your shrine and renew your center. Again, meditate for a time on the whole work: on the grove, and the spirits and especially on your own Pagan path.

[16] Closing

[17] Ground and center

Appendices

[A] Recommended Reading Lists
[B] Dedicant Path Documentation
[C] Adapting the DP to Specific Ethnic Paths
[D] Dedicant Path for Grove Building
[E] Rune and Ogham Charts

Appendix A:

Recommended Reading Lists

The Dedicant's Reading List

The Pagan revival has been troubled from the beginning by shoddy scholarship and indulgence in esoteric fantasy. When wishful thinking and poor science take the place of true knowledge, all of Paganism is harmed. Ár nDraíocht Féin was founded on the principle of respect for the actual old ways of Europe. We believe that by starting with the foundational remains of Iron Age Paganism we can build a modern system that will serve modern needs and be true to ancestral spirit.

We recommend you choose one or two titles at a time and begin working your way through them. This is by no means exhaustive, but is the initial list of books that ADF Dedicants must choose from, and thus consists mainly of books for a student beginning to study Paganism the first time. There is little direct mythology for each culture because we hope to have our Dedicants understand the culture that the myths come out of before delving directly into the myths.

We've also worked hard to make sure that every book on this list is in print. Unfortunately, all the best books seem to go out of print, and sometimes libraries don't carry them. We hope this list will not only aid study, but will also be highly accessible, and we have broken the list into the following categories: Indo-European Studies; Hearth Cultures: Celtic Culture, Greek/Hellenic Culture, Norse Culture, Proto-Indo-European Culture, Roman Culture, Slavic/Baltic Culture, Vedic Culture; Pagan Revival; Nature Awareness; Additional Notes; and Other Listings.

INDO-EUROPEAN STUDIES & OVERVIEW

In Search of the Indo-Europeans: Language, Archaeology, and Myth: [978-0500276167] by
J.P. Mallory.
A summary of known scholarship on the peoples from whom the Celts, Germans, Greco-Roman, and Baltic cultures descended. This book is fairly dense and reads on an advanced level. It could also be classed as Proto-Indo-European. (We have a short review of this book available on our website.)
Reading Level: Late Undergraduate to post-Graduate

Comparative Mythology: [978-0801839382] by Jaan Puhvel.
   A good discussion of Indo-European myth. It covers the entire spectrum of Indo-European myth.
   Reading Level: Post-Graduate

A History of Pagan Europe: [978-0415158046] by Prudence Jones.
   A simpler review of the history of Pagan peoples and their beliefs.
   Reading Level: Early Undergraduate

The Myth of Matriarchal Prehistory: Why an Invented Past Will Not Give Women a Future: [978-0807067932] by Cynthia Eller.
   This book takes a hard look at what evidence there is or is not for the Gimbutas assertion of a matriarchal goddess-worshipping, pan-European Neolithic society.
   Reading Level: Late High School to Early College

CELTIC CULTURE

There is no definitive collection of Celtic myth, but there are many good sources on who the Celts were, including a few mythical cycles:

The Celtic Heroic Age: Literary Sources for Ancient Celtic Europe and Early Ireland and Wales: [978-1891271090] by John T. Koch (Editor).
   This book includes a large number of sources on the Celts, all included in a single place. Many of the translations are updated, and it includes many obscure texts.
   Reading Level: Late High School to Early College

Celtic Heritage: Ancient Tradition in Ireland and Wales: [978-0500270394] by Alwyn and Brinley Rees.
   The very best study of pattern and meaning in Celtic myth, with special reference to Vedic lore.
   Reading Level: Late Undergraduate to post-Graduate

Pagan Celtic Britain: [978-0897334358] by Anne Ross.
   An exhaustive survey of known archaeology and lore about Celtic remains in England, Scotland and Wales.
   Reading Level: Late Undergraduate to post-Graduate

The Mabinogi, and Other Medieval Welsh Tales: [978-0520253964] by Patrick K. Ford. The most academically accepted translation, it also includes the Battle of the Trees, a pronunciation guide, and an index of names.
   Reading Level: Undergraduate

The Tain: Translated from the Irish Epic Tain Bo Cuailnge: [978-0192803733] by Thomas Kinsella, Trans.
   One of the main Irish Myths, the Ulster Cycle is key to understanding Irish mythology. This translation is considered standard among academics.
   Reading Level: Middle School

A Brief History of the Druids: [978-0786709878] by Peter Beresford Ellis.
: The best modern survey of what we know and don't know about the Celtic Druids. (previously/also marketed as "The Druids")
Reading Level: Post-Graduate

The Druids: [978-0500273630] by Stuart Piggott.
: Previously the best survey. Somewhat unfriendly to the culture it describes, but full of good data about the archeology and facts about the Druids.
Reading Level: Post-Graduate

Greek/Hellenic Culture

Hellenic Pagan lore is contained in a number of books, available in inexpensive student editions:

Greek Religion: [978-0631156246] by Walter Burkett.
: An overall survey of Cult and practice in Greek Paganism, and is a basic text book of beliefs.
Reading Level: Late Undergraduate to post-Graduate

Religion in the Ancient Greek City: [978-0521423571] by Louise Bruit Zaidman, Pauline Schmitt Pantel; Paul Cartledge (Trans.)
: Another good overall summary of Greek religious practice.
Reading Level: Post-Graduate

Theogony and Works and Days: [978-0192839411] by Hesiod, with M. L. West, ed.
: Descriptions of both myths and religious practices.
The introduction to Norman O. Brown's translation is considered to be one of the best, though his translation is somewhat dated.
Reading Level: Late Undergraduate to post-Graduate

The Iliad and The Odyssey or The Homeric Hymns: [978-0801879838] by Homer.
: These tales embody much important lore about Hellenic Paganism. The Hymns make the powers and nature of each of the deities clear.
Reading Level: High School

Norse Culture

The Poetic Edda: [978-0292764996] by Lee M. Hollander, Edda Saemundar, eds.
: The Eddas, in addition to the Sagas, make up many of our primary sources for the Norse traditions. Hollander's translation is currently regarded as the best in academic circles, but it is more difficult to read than some others.
Reading Level: College

Edda: by Snorri Sturluson, Anthony Faulkes, eds.
: This is also known as "The Prose Edda", because it is related but different from the Poetic Edda above. While the Prose Edda was discovered before the Poetic Edda, scholars have come to date the former as historically later than the latter. However, both Eddas are useful, interesting, and widely cited in Norse scholarship. The Everyman edition (linked here) is the complete Prose Edda - some editions leave out valuable material.
Reading Level: Mostly late High School; Introduction: Post-Graduate

Gods and Myths of Northern Europe: [978-0140136272] by H.R. Ellis-Davidson.
   Davidson is one of the best writers on northern European Paganism. All her books are worth reading.
   Reading Level: College

The Saga of the Volsungs: The Norse Epic of Sigurd the Dragon Slayer: [978-0141026411] by Jesse L. Byock.
   Akin to the Nibelungenlied, this book more accurately reflects the Pagan ideals in the literature, rather than the courtly nature of the Ring Saga, and is preferred for DP work. The introduction here is almost as valuble as the Saga itself.
   Reading Level: Middle School to early High School

Myths and Symbols in Pagan Europe: Early Scandinavian and Celtic Religions: [978-0815624417] by H.R. Ellis-Davidson.
   A good shore compilation of what is really known and what can be surmised of the religions of the ancient Celts and Germans.
   Reading Level: College

PROTO-INDO-EUROPEAN CULTURE

Deep Ancestors: Practicing the Religion of the Proto-Indo-Europeans: [978-0976568131] by Ceisiwr Serith, ADF Publishing.
   This book provides a solid introduction to Proto-Indo-European work and lays an excellent framework for work in "common Indo-European" formats. Included here are rituals for the turning wheel of the year, from planting to harvest to equinox rites. Additionally, there are rites for ancestors, lists of reconstructed deity names (and the functions those names imply), and domestic rituals for the family at their hearth.
   Reading Level: Late High School

ROMAN CULTURE

Romans and Their Gods in the Age of Augustus: [978-0393005431] by R.M. Ogilvie. Ogilvie's brief text on this subject has been the definitive text on Roman religion for decades. He demonstrates his thorough understanding of how the Romans worshipped, as well as how they thought about their religion during the Age of Augustus.
   Reading Level: Late Undergraduate to post-Graduate

Fasti: [978-0140446906] by Ovid.
   A poetic description of the festivals of the Roman year which unfortunately breaks off at the end of June. This classic work is available from many publishers. Try searching at Amazon.com to find the price range or book style that you prefer.
   Reading Level: Middle School

The Gods of Ancient Rome: Religion in Everyday Life from Archaic to Imperial Times: [978-0415929745] by Robert Turcan; Antonia Nevell, trans.
   A good source for Roman religion. It seems that his books are being translated slowly, so keep an eye out for them.
   Reading Level: Late High School to early Undergraduate

<u>An Introduction to Roman Religion</u>: [978-0253216601] by John Scheid; Janet Lloyd, trans.
  This book comes highly recommended as an intro to the religion of this culture.
  Reading Level: Late Undergraduate to post-Graduate

<u>Handbook to Life in Ancient Rome</u>: [978-0816050260] by Lesley Adkins, Roy A. Adkins.
  Focuses mainly on culture, but there is also some information on Roman religion.
  Reading Level: High School

SLAVIC/BALTIC CULTURE

<u>The Bath House at Midnight: Magic in Russia (Magic in History)</u>: [978-0750921114] by W.F. Ryan.
  A collection of scholarly literature on the history of magic and divination in Russia. Information was gathered by the author for over 30 years.
  Reading Level: Post-Graduate

<u>The Early Slavs: Culture & Society in Early Medieval Eastern Europe</u>: [978-0801439773] by P.M. Barford.
  An easy to read and nicely objective introduction to early Slavic culture.
  Reading Level: Post-Graduate

<u>Russian Myths</u>: [978-0292791589] by Elizabeth Warner.
  An overview of the customs and themes underlying Russian beliefs.
  Reading Level: Late Undergraduate

VEDIC CULTURE

<u>Religion and Philosophy of the Veda and Upanishads (2 Volumes)</u>: [978-8120806443] by A.B. Keith.
  This is the must have book for anyone interested in Vedism. While Keith does not focus on much of the material that should be dealt with for a practitioner of Vedism, he does introduce those new to Vedism with strong facts and a wonderful starting point.
  Reading Level: Post-Graduate

<u>Religion of the Veda</u>: [978-8120803923] by Hermann Oldenberg; Shridhar B. Shrotri (Trans.)
  Oldenberg does often get confused on some Vedic concepts, as pointed out by out noted scholars such as Keith and Macdonell, but this is a must read for further understanding the ancient Vedics.
  Reading Level: Post-Graduate

<u>The Origins and Development of Classical Hinduism</u>: [978-0195073492] by A. L. Basham
  This book focuses primarily on Classical Hinduism but it does cover the Vedic period and it's disintegration into Hinduism. This is a wonderful introduction which allows the individual to see the differences between the Indo-European Vedism and the non Indo-European Hinduism.
  Reading Level: College

Vedic Mythology: [978-0548609132] by Arthur Anthony Macdonell.
This book is a must have for anyone serious about Vedism. It describes a large group of the Gods, complete with references from the Vedas and just where to find these references yourself.
Reading Level: Late Undergraduate to post-Graduate

MODERN PAGANISM & THE PAGAN REVIVAL

Drawing Down the Moon: Witches, Druids, Goddess-Worshippers, and Other Pagans in America Today: [978-0143038191] by Margot Adler.
The classic survey of American Neopaganism, including plenty on ADF, our origins and growth.
Reading Level: College

The Triumph of the Moon: A History of Modern Pagan Witchcraft: [978-0192854490] by Ronald Hutton.
A detailed book, discussing the origins of Wicca, the source of most of Neo-Paganism. It serves as a counter-balance to much of the information and theories that are likely to be encountered when reviewing Neo-Paganism in general. It is recommended that, due to its focus on Wicca, Dedicants supplement this reading with more sources.
Reading Level: Late Undergraduate to Post-Graduate

Being a Pagan: Druids, Wiccans, and Witches Today: [978-0892819041] by Ellen Evert Hopman, Lawrence Bond.
This book is a set of interviews from modern Neo-Pagans. Some ADF members are interviewed for this book, as well. (Also marketed as: People of the Earth: The New Pagans Speak Out)
Reading Level: Late Undergraduate to Post-Graduate

The Idiot's Guide to Paganism: [978-0028642666] by Carl McColman.
A book that covers the basic forms of modern Paganism.
Reading Level: Late High School to Early Undergraduate

Her Hidden Children: The Rise of Wicca And Paganism in America: [978-0759102026] by Chas S. Clifton.
A book covering the basics of the Neo-Pagan movement today, starting with Wicca and exploring the varieties of Paganism from there.
Reading Level: Late Undergraduate to post-Graduate

NATURE AWARENESS

Note: These books do not fulfill a requirement for the ADF Dedicant Path, but are provided to help Dedicants work through the Nature Awareness section of the DP.

Landscape and Memory: [978-0679735120] by Simon Schama.
An extraordinary survey of European attitudes to and conceptualizations of nature over the course of the last 500 years or so, and how our ideas of nature have shaped how we interact with it. Spans Europe from Poland to the Atlantic and from England to the Mediterranean, as well as (the European experience of) America and Australia. Reasonably scholarly but still quite readable.

<u>Keeping a Nature Journal</u>: Discover a Whole New Way of Seeing the World Around You: [978-1580174930] by Clare Walker Leslie; Charles E. Roth.
A very popular book with homeschoolers and teachers.

Additional Notes

We recommend that the beginning student avoid any nonfiction by Robert Graves, D.J. Conway, Lewis Spense, H.P. Blavatsky, Edward Williams (aka Iolo Morganwg), or any works by others based on their writings, or those of Merlin Stone, Barbara Walker, or other revisionist ideologues. Some of the assertions made in these sources can't be supported by current scholarship on the Druids; the use of common sense and a critical eye are highly recommended in dealing with these books (and all the other books listed on this page as well).

This is not to say that they don't have their own possible worth or that people shouldn't know about these books, but that an understanding of these writers should come after understanding Druidry/Neopaganism in general. One has to get a firm grounding, four walls and a roof before she can decide on what kinds of curtains to look at.

When in doubt, consult your nearest tree…

Additional Reading Resources

These resources are not required to work the Dedicant Path nor can they be used for the book reviews you will need to submit to document your work on the Dedicant Path (unless they are also listed above). These books, especially those in the first section that deal specifically with ADF's own flavor of Druidy, are listed in order to help our students grow and learn what the Druid Path is all about, while giving them both the grounding in history and the ritual knowledge needed to deepen the work on this path.

BOOKS ABOUT OUR OWN DRUIDRY

<u>A Book of Pagan Prayer</u>: [978-1578632558] by Ceisiwr Serith – Recommended for anyone interested in a serious study of Our Druidry.

<u>Bonewits Essential Guide to Druidry</u>: [978-0806527109] by Isaac Bonewits

<u>The Solitary Druid</u>: [978-0806526751] by Robert "Skip" Ellison

<u>Sacred Fire, Holy Well</u>: [978-0976568124] by Ian Corrigan

<u>The Druid's Alphabet</u>: [978-1594055034] by Robert "Skip" Ellison

OVERVIEWS OF EUROPEAN PAGANISM

<u>The History of Pagan Europe</u>: [978-0415158046] by Pennick and Jones

<u>From Olympus to Camelot</u>: The World of European Mythology by David Leeming

OVERVIEWS OF SPECIFIC CULTURAL SYSTEMS

<u>Deep Ancestors – Practicing the Religion of the Proto-Indo-Europeans</u>: [978-0976568131] by Ceisiwr Serith

Magic of the Celtic Gods and Goddesses: [978-1564147837] by Carl McColman

The Complete Idiot's Guide to Celtic Wisdom: [978-0028644172] by Carl McColman

Exploring the Northern Tradition: [978-1564147912] by Galina Krasskova

Mysteries of Demeter: [978-1578631414] by Jennifer Reif

RITUAL AND DEVOTIONAL SUPPORT

A Book of Pagan Prayer: [978-1578632558] by Ceisiwr Serith

A Circle of Stones: [978-1573531061] by Erynn Laurie

Creating Circles and Ceremonies: [978-1564148643] by Oberon and Morning Glory Ravenheart-Zell

MEDITATION AND ALTERED STATES OF AWARENESS

Monsters and Magical Sticks: There's No Such Thing as Hypnosis [978-1561840267] by Steven Heller

Prometheus Rising: [978-1561840564] by Robert Anton Wilson

OGHAM AND RUNES

The Druid's Alphabet: [978-1594055034] by Robert "Skip" Ellison

Taking Up The Runes: [978-1578633258] by Diana Paxson

THEOLOGY

A World Full of Gods: [978-0976568100] by John Michael Greer

The Deities Are Many: [978-0791463888] by Jordan D. Paper

Pagan Theology: [978-0814797082] by Michael York

BOOKS ABOUT OTHER FORMS OF MODERN DRUIDRY

The Druid Renaissance: [978-1855384804] by Phillip Carr-Gomm, ed.

The Druidry Handbook: Spiritual Practice Rooted in the Living Earth: [978-1578633548] by John Michael Greer

The Mysteries of Druidry: [978-1564148780] by Brendan "Cathbad" Myers

Appendix B:

Dedicant Path Documentation

This guide offers you the details of the Dedicant's Path–the ongoing skills of Druidic Paganism that will serve you throughout your spiritual life. The Ar nDraiocht Fein Dedicant's Program is the documentation of the work of the Path, a task of writing and notating that allows our distant leadership to be certain that a student is doing the work. The Dedicant's Path provides important primary training for those who wish to begin the real work of Druidic spirituality. The Dedicant Program provides the entry-level essays and documentation that admits students to our further training programs.

Many students may find the Dedicant Path to be all they need to keep our Druidic spiritual way in their own lives. If they continue in their program of study, virtue and piety, they can find a variety of directions for further growth. These students may not care to document their efforts, or have the formal recognition of ADF's Druidic Order for their work.

Those who wish to continue their work in our training programs, working towards Initiate status, and perhaps eventual clergy ordination, or those who wish their work in the Path to be formally recognized by our Order will need to complete and submit the formal written documentation of the program.

The documentation is to be submitted to the ADF Preceptor, or to one's local Grove's Senior Druid, or to one of our fully ordained Clergy.

The following are the guidelines for minimum standards for completion of the Dedicant Program documentation for the purposes of gaining entry to the ADF Study Programs:

Required Documentation

1. Written discussions of the Dedicant's understanding of each of the following nine virtues: wisdom, piety, vision, courage, integrity, perseverance, hospitality, moderation and fertility. The Dedicant may also include other virtues, if desired, and compare them to these nine. (125 words minimum each)

2. Short essays on each of the eight ADF High Days including a discussion of the meaning of each feast. (125 words minimum each)

3. Short book reviews on at least: 1 Indo-European studies title, 1 preferred ethnic study title and 1 modern Paganism title. These titles can be selected from the recommended reading list in the Dedicant Program manual or the ADF web site, or chosen by the student, with prior approval of the Preceptor. (325 word minimum each)

4. A brief description, with photos if possible, of the Dedicant's home shrine and plans for future improvements. (150 words minimum)

5. An essay focusing on the Dedicants understanding of the meaning of the "Two Powers" meditation or other form of 'grounding and centering', as used in meditation and ritual. This account should include impressions and insights that the Dedicant gained from practical experience. (300 word minimum)

6. An essay or journal covering the Dedicant's personal experience of building mental discipline, through the use of meditation, trance, or other systematic techniques on a regular basis. The experiences in the essay or journal should cover at least a five months period. (800 words minimum)

7. An account of the Dedicant's efforts to work with nature, honor the Earth, and understand the impacts and effects of the Dedicant's lifestyle choices on the environment and/or the local ecosystem and how she or he could make a difference to the environment on a local level. (500 word minimum)

8. A brief account of each High Day ritual attended or performed by the Dedicant in a twelve month period. High Days attended/performed might be celebrated with a local grove, privately, or with another Neopagan group. At least 4 of the rituals attended/performed during the training period must be ADF-style. (100 words minimum each)

9. ONE essay describing the Dedicants understanding of and relationship to EACH of the Three Kindred: the Spirits of Nature, the Ancestors and the Gods. (300 words minimum for each Kindred and 1000 words total)

10. A brief account of the efforts of the Dedicant to develop and explore a personal (or Grove-centered) spiritual practice, drawn from a specific culture or combination of cultures. (600 words minimum)

11. The text of the Dedicant's Oath Rite and a self-evaluation of the Dedicant's performance of the rite. (500 word minimum)

Writing A Book Review

Because we've been frequently asked, we include these guidelines.

Book reviews may be typed or handwritten, but the 1-2 pages requirement refers specifically to pretty standard format: typewritten, double-spaced, one-inch margins, using a size 12 point like Times New Roman. That works out to roughly 325-350 words per page.

Be sure your name appears in the top, right-hand corner of each page, and as a heading include whether this is the Indo-European studies, the ethnic study, or the modern paganism study, then the bibliographical information. (None of this is included in the word count, by the way!)

Within the body of your review, you should at least:

1. Explain who or what the book is about. Generally, and in your own words, write a paragraph or two as if you were writing the blurb for the inside jacket, describing for a friend or co-worker what you are reading, or if you were asked to write a summary for amazon.com.

2. Explain the significance of this book. There may be hundreds of books on similar subjects—or none. What do you think was so utterly compelling about this topic to the author that s/he would undertake years of research, writing and editing to share this information with folks like you? Perhaps as importantly, explain why you think ADF chose that particular book as required reading for its Dedicants—what significance does it have in Our Own Druidry?

3. Explain the significance of the book to you, personally. Maybe you were profoundly affected by this book; after reading it you perceive the world around in an entirely new way. Maybe you thought it was the best sleep aid since Sominex and now use it for a doorstop. Probably, you fall somewhere in between these two scenarios. You could describe in the passages or points that struck you most profoundly; ideas you found surprising, offensive or questionable; concepts that helped clarify ideas you have had floating around in your head for years, yet never have been able to explain. This is the most important part of your review and requires some very thoughtful reflection.

4. Explain why or why not you would recommend this book to others. Did you enjoy reading it? Was it difficult, but worth the effort (or not)? Are there any cautions or biases you would want to be sure you told others about?

Although it should probably go without saying, ADF will not tolerate any form of plagiarism, whether intentional or inadvertent. When writing a book review, it is a good idea to set the book aside entirely, jot down or type your thoughts and ideas, and only when you have your notes or preliminary draft completed, refer back to the book for specific details or quotes. As with any academic writing, direct quotes must be clearly marked as such, with footnotes or parenthetical references to the page from which they were taken.

The Journal

Or "Look, just do it…"

There is one traditional technique of study and progress in skill that we cannot recommend firmly enough, and that is the journal. The regular recording of your efforts and their results is one of the most valuable habits you will ever develop as a Druidic student. There are many ways to use journaling, from deep introspection to simple note-taking. In this case we're recommending the keeping of notes and records on as much of your ritual, meditation and reading work as you can.

There is no single annoying chore that will make you thank yourself later quite so much as journaling. Sure some people like it for its own sake… but for many of us it is enough just to prepare for a ritual or exercise and execute it – the follow-up task of recording the work and results just never quite happens. We can't recommend enough that you make whatever amount of effort you can to record your work. Like any part of our practices, it is better to do a little journaling than to do none, better to do more than do a little– all a matter of degree.

So choose a simple notebook or blank book or, if you favor the keyboard, create your journal in your favorite program, or open some journaling account on the web. The advantage of a book, perhaps, is that you can set it by or on your shrine or working space, to remind you of your commitment to it. It can be taken to forests and seashores with little risk of technical failure, and requires no power source. Your Author has an affection for handwriting in books–I feel it is a step closer to the old memorization–more somatic, more personal. Still the e-journal is working well for many of our students.

Many students of Our Druidry will choose to do the documentation and formal practice that we call the Dedicants Program. The Program is a way to demonstrate to our organization that you have the basics of the skills and understandings we hope to teach through the Druid's Path. In order to allow students spread over the world to have their work recognized, we ask for written reports on your efforts. If you start your journal from your first rituals and experiments you'll later find yourself with a solid base of material to work with. To repeat, you'll thank yourself for work done in these early stages. Not only will it support any later formal writing efforts, it will give you invaluable material on which to reflect as you move along the Druid's Path.

So, look–just do it. Get a book, open an account. Do a little, do a lot… just do the journal!

What to Record in Your Journal:

- The date, location and intention of any Druidic ritual or meditative exercise you perform. If possible, write a short summary of how you felt as a result, and any other outcomes you find important.

- A record of the divinations you may do or omen that you take, and notes toward your understanding of the symbol system you're using

- Notes on the High Days, their meaning and symbolism, as you do the preparation for each day.

- Notes on the books you read–name, author, subject and a few words on your reaction to the book.

- Notes on your understanding of the Nine Virtues, as they occur to you or as they arise in your work.

- Notes on your understanding of the Three Kindreds as you begin to work with them, and as they become more aware of you.

- Notes on the land on which you live–land and water, air and resources.

- Some of these are things you must record while memory is fresh, but you can spend time just talking to yourself by writing about your understanding of Our Druidry.

- Plan to make an entry at least once per week in your journal. Such an entry should include any rituals or meditations you worked that week, and any other topic on which you might write some musings.

Appendix C:

Adapting the Dedicant's Path to Specific Ethnic Paths

ADF is a family of local religions, united by the common basis of Indo-European cosmology, and our modern practice. Many come to Our Druidry interested in pursuing the spiritual work of a specific Indo-European ethnicity. Celtic, Norse, Hellenic, Baltic and Slavic ways have all been worked by ADF members and Groves over the years.

The articles in this handbook can be described as having a certain Celtic bias. The authors have come primarily from Celtic paths, and, while effort has been made to be inclusive of other traditions, some students may feel a need to tailor the work more specifically to the culture in which they seek to work. So, we provide a few ideas. These should probably be acceptable to any preceptor you may be working under, but it is best to review changes with the preceptor, if you mean to work for formal ADF recognition.

1. **Virtues**: can be adapted per the lore of each culture, though our set of nine covers a lot of general IE bases.

2. **Piety**: Specific calendars can be described. Ask your preceptor about adapting your practice to specific cultural calendars.

3. **Study**: Specific book lists. Also, this is the section where we have included general cosmology. A good bit of this general cosmology applies to most IE cultures –even land sea and sky is a constant, anywhere that isn't landlocked. But ethnic specialty sections could be written–even a specifically Irish or Gaulish cosmology would differ in detail from the general ideas given.

4. **Home Shrine**: The process of establishing a shrine is pretty general. If there are specific items proper for a culture, those could be used and described. Most importantly for this section, devotions need to be written in ways that reflect any special cosmological and ritual patterns, and patterns of spirits in the culture. See ADF on-line for a growing list of specific ethnic rites and devotions.

5. **Mental Training**: Probably pretty general, regardless of culture.

6. **Nature Attunement**: Again, pretty general - specific ethnic customs about greeting the spirits would be useful.

7. **Full Ritual**: We define ADF ritual as ritual which follows our Order of Ritual, at least in its broad outline. Our Order of Ritual has a lot of leeway, and does a good job of adapting Indo-European ideas into a working ritual environment. Students may develop specific ethnic adaptations of the OoR, both for solitaries and for groups. Please check your ideas with your preceptor.

8. **Hearth Religion**: Every culture contains lore on what Pagans do for personal religion.

9. **Oath**: Adapt as inspired by the culture

Appendix D:

Using the DP for Grove Building

As ADF grows into our next stage, we hope to offer more and better instruction in the basics of our Druidic religions. The first stage of that instruction has been published as the Dedicant's work, a set of articles meant to introduce basic spiritual skills. The work was designed primarily for individual students, working alone if need be.

Dedicant work can also be a guide for the building of an ADF Grove. With a little adaptation the work can help the founding members of a Grove learn our symbolism and rites, and begin building the spiritual content that will indwell the new worship circle.

This short article will suggest some uses of the program for developing a new Grove.

The Three Triads of the Dedicants' Work

Lifetime Commitments

1. **Virtue**: the student commits to seeking virtue in their life.
2. **Piety**: the student commits to keeping the observances of the way.
3. **Study**: the student commits to learning all they can about the facts of the Old Ways.

Devotion, and Training The Mind

1. **The Home Shrine**: the student begins their own Hearth religion, by establishing a shrine.
2. **Meditation, Energy Work and Trance**: the student practices mental relaxation and stillness, the Two Currents or something like it, and learns basic trance skills
3. **Nature & Kindred Attunements**: the student seeks to understand the local environment, and to begin to be aware of the Spirits within it.

Ritual and Dedication

1 **Full Ritual Worship**: the student learns and practices the ADF Order of Ritual in personal and small-group seasonal rites.

2 **Hearth Religion**: the student chooses a traditional culture in which to work, and begins relationship with specific Gods & Spirits.

3 **Dedicant's Oath**: the student proclaims their achievement, and their commitment to the Druid's Way

Getting Started and Making a Commitment

The first triad of the Dedicant's work offers a new group the opportunity to clarify their ideas and their direction. They make commitments to each other, and to the spiritual work of Pagan Druidism.

The order of the Dedicant's work is somewhat arbitrary and conventional. In using the work for group development it might be best to begin with the concept of Piety.

Piety

A Grove cannot be built by a single person. Even when one individual provides the moving and directing spirit of a group, there must be at least two others who put their names to the founding documents of a Grove. The best situation is when the three founding members of the group are all equally involved in the invention and development of the new organization.

The virtue of piety is about keeping faith, about keeping commitment to specific practices and works over a long period of time. Those who commit to a Grove's work will be involved in working public rites every six weeks, year after year, as well as holding or attending other rites and meetings. So a new group might begin by choosing to commit to attendance at a Dedicant's training circle.

The founding group of three or more might choose to make an agreement to view their work as an experiment, with a specific time commitment. Of course we would like all of our Grove organizing teams to be prepared for a lifetime commitment to Druidry and to ADF, but we know that to be less than reasonable. Organizers are more likely to approve our work on a kind of trial basis, and to take an experimental attitude to our doctrines and works. In many ways this is a good thing. Those who commit after a period of trial may be more likely to stay committed.

To get a sense of the pace of Grove organizing, a training circle should commit to meeting at least twice monthly, and perhaps more. The circle might decide on a time-limit for the first experimental commitment. If the members (3 or more) can tolerate a full year's involvement, they should conclude that year ready to work well as a public Grove. Other groups may choose a shorter initial experiment, perhaps six months or even three.

This initial group can choose to take the First Oath together, as a mutual commitment.

It is important for a training circle to discuss, early in their process, how they will handle new members. One of the most important policies for any ADF Grove is that they must be open and inclusive. A Grove is not a coven - it must be able to operate even when the group is less than like-minded. Membership in a Grove cannot be contingent on a personality compatibility between new members and the existing membership. All interested persons of good will and honest intentions must be welcomed into a working Grove.

In a new study circle there may be an inclination to limit the group to the founders, or to a certain early list of members. This can be a useful technique for the first few months, perhaps. It is, however, strongly advised that a new training circle be prepared to seek and be open to new members as quickly as feasible. The founding group should become accustomed to accepting and integrating new members, a task they will hopefully need to continue throughout the life of the Grove.

In setting a meeting schedule for their first commitment, the group might also set a target date for their first public ceremony. An ADF Grove is defined by commitment to providing open, public rites to its local Pagan community. In many ways this is the primary mission of a Grove, the core of the effort to build a Pagan institution that can serve a larger community. By choosing a target date for the first public rite the founding group is given a fairly short term goal for which to prepare. A date of six months to a year from the first meetings might be reasonable, perhaps sooner for groups with members who have ritual experience from other systems.

Content of Early Meetings–Virtue & Study

It can be interesting and productive for a new group to discuss their impressions of the basic lists of Pagan virtues offered in the Dedicant articles. Members can write their journal entries on each virtue and share them with one another. Members will thus get to know one another's ideas, share insights and perhaps uncover important issues in the Grove's new work. Members may also discover or clarify where they fit in the model of the Three Functions–Wise Ones, Warriors and Providers.

ADF Does not intend to impose any one list of Pagan virtues on our members or Groves. We do mean to recommend that all of our lives and work be based on the idea of virtue, and that we draw that virtue from the lore and wisdom of ancient Paganism. It may be that local Groves will develop their own sets of virtues, that can be taught along with national and traditional versions.

It might be interesting for a training circle to condense their understanding of the virtues into a single poem, song or invocation. As well as focusing that understanding, this would provide a valuable piece of ritual speech for future work.

ADF's work has been and must be based on direct study of reputable scholastic sources, combined with earnest aspiration to the flow of poetic wisdom and inspiration. In order for inspiration to have its greatest value it must have a full supply of solid information with which to interact. Scholarship is the hardwood fuel in which the spark of inspiration catches, the pure mash in which the leaven of inspiration works.

One of the first tasks of a new training circle is to begin systematic reading and discussion of the works on the reading list. The training circle might choose to have all members read the same book at the same time, discussing chapters at meetings. Alternately, students may read different books and report on them to one another. Whichever, the goal is for all members to read a minimum of three solid books during their Dedicant training, at least one of them an introduction to Indo-European comparative mythology. It should also be said that three books is the absolute minimum that should be read. In this case more is certainly better.

One of the central considerations at this stage is the question of a new Grove's ethnic focus. ADF encourages each Grove to choose a specific cultural complex on which to build their work. As a new group gathers this focus may, or may not, be obvious. Some new Groves coalesce around a desire to work a specific culture's mysteries, drawn by the call of the Gael or the Norse or some other Indo-European way. Others are drawn by ADF's commitment to public Paganism, or our ceremonial patterns, and have members interested in several IE paths.

If a training circle can agree early on the cultural focus of their work, they have a considerable advantage. The group can begin to systematically study their culture of choice with excursions into related cultures for depth and support. If no focus is apparent immediately, the circle should study broadly, work to find their personal Patrons, and expect that, along the way, they will also find the cultural path that will suit their Grove.

In this first step we find a group of students meeting regularly to discuss ideas and study. In many groups this might be enough for a first phase. Other groups may wish to begin immediately with the practices in part two, as well.

Training the Mind and Attuning to the Powers.

Meditation and Energy Work: The work of training the mind is the foundation on which all spiritual practice is built. The Dedicant's material places considerable emphasis on these techniques, and a new training circle should, too.

Any and all of the meditations in the Dedicant's work can be directly adapted for group practice. Silent meditation might be practiced with a timer, beginning with three or five minutes and working up to fifteen to twenty.

The scripts for the Two Powers meditations, or the basic trance induction, might be read by one member onto tape and played back. There could be an advantage in having the members take turns reading the scripts, allowing each to develop skill in guiding trances.

In that context, a word should be said about critiques and evaluations. It is always ADF's goal to help our members improve their skills and abilities. To that end we encourage Grove members to ask one another to criticize and examine the work done by members. Likewise we ask ourselves to be open to honest criticism, and willing to adjust our style and methods to the needs of those with whom we work. A study circle should be a place where all efforts will be appreciated, but also where these efforts may be analyzed and dissected. Those who wish to stand forward as presenters, ritualists and artists in our work need to be prepared for gentle, thoughtful criticism.

Here is a simple outline for a group guided meditation session.

1. **Musical signal**: a chime, perhaps, struck three or nine times.
2. **Rhythmic breathing**: all practice the complete breath together, perhaps with one member counting the first few breaths. Nine breaths together is enough.
3. **Silent meditation**: perhaps with a timer, perhaps with a monitor, who rings a chime when the time is done.
4. **Two Powers**: one member reads the induction, or extemporizes. (Add other group exercises here as skill increases)
5. **Musical signal**: to indicate the end of the exercise.

Steps one through three can be completed in just a few minutes with a new group. Once the group is doing five to seven minutes of silent meditation, or more, they might go on to Two Powers work, extending the length of the silent work as they gain intensity in the energy work.

This work will provide good opportunity for discussion and material for formal journal entries. Unlike performance skills, the results of meditation are a very individual matter. The circle should be open and accepting of descriptions of meditative and internal events. Critical judgement should not be abandoned, however. If a member begins transmitting orders from a Goddess, or whatever, their claims should be tested and judged.

It is suggested that early exercises be kept to a specific length of time. There may be a tendency to want to sit in meditation indefinitely, but this should be avoided. The willed act of entering an altered state, staying there, then ending it through will is an important lesson in itself.

The Shrine–Beginning Devotional Work.

As individual members begin to establish their home shrines, the new Grove has the opportunity to gather their first set of ritual objects.

The Grove's approach to beginning ritual work will depend on the experience and skill-level of the members. Those who are making their first efforts at Pagan ceremony should probably follow the outline of training closely. Beginning with simple meditation, the group adds the shrine and the Simple Devotion, and works up to simple versions of the Order of Ritual. A training circle with members that have solid previous ritual experience might choose to work more quickly toward the Order of Ritual. Unless, however, they are trained in ADF's symbolism and ways, they might still do well to work through each step in order.

In any case, creating the new Grove's first group shrine should be an exciting and creative process. Assembling the tools and hallows can combine the group's scholastic work with their inspiration. It is a way of beginning to manifest the group mind of the Grove, and of planting a physical seed from which the grove's spiritual work can grow.

The shrine should be focused around symbols of the Sacred Center. Many Groves use the Fire, Well & Tree as a triple complex of the center. This is recommended, though not required. The circle will need to consider whether to begin by creating 'tabletop' versions of the Hallows, or starting out immediately with a set large enough for larger group ritual. There are advantages to both.

Beginning with an 'altar-top' set insures that the Grove will have proper tools for a small-group working. Larger group rites do require large tools that can draw the eye of many participants. In smaller groups these can be clumsy and burdensome; a smaller-scaled set may serve better. Creating a small set of hallows can also help the Grove decide on what they want for their larger items.

A small set of indoor ritual items might consist of:

1. **Fire**: A wooden or ceramic platter, approximately 12" in diameter, on which are placed a ring of nine small candles (the kind called 'tea lights' are ideal). In the center of the ring of candles is placed a small censer or fire-bowl, in which fire offerings are burned.

2. **Well**: A metal or ceramic cauldron. A fist-sized vessel should be a good size.

3. **Tree**: A straight branch (perhaps forked, or three-tined) of a proper wood, no more than approximately 18" long, fastened securely to a base that will allow it to stand firmly. Some branches may fit comfortably into a candle-holder.

A nail can be driven up through the bottom of a wooden base of the kind sold to display knick-knacks. The branch is then fastened to that nail. The Tree can then be decorated as the group sees fit.

To these should be added: Two or three good quality drinking vessels, for pouring offerings and drinking blessing. A vessel as large or larger than the Well to receive poured offerings. Perhaps a white cloth to place on the floor or tabletop, on which to place the Hallows, decorated as the Grove pleases. Several small dishes and vessels to hold offerings as they wait to be given.

If the group wishes, this can all be arranged on a low table that can serve as an 'altar' This might be especially proper to those Groves working, for example, a Hellenic system in which altars are traditional. Other I.E. systems seem not to have used altar type tables. In that case the white cloth might be placed directly on the earth. The Tree is then placed in its center and the hallows arranged around it in a pattern symbolically meaningful to the members. That process can, in itself, help the new Grove to clarify their mutual understanding of the powers represented by the Fire, Well & Tree.

There are several small-group devotions and simple rites available to new groups. The Simple Devotion in the Dedicant articles can be adapted, and a new script is provided in an appendix to this article. The Simple Rite of Offering could be used by a new group fairly quickly as its language and gestures are elementary.

Study circles may find it valuable to begin by reciting the rites in unison, with various individuals performing the actions. That allows each to begin learning the text of the rite, relieves one person of all the work of recitation, and helps to build the group mind. On the other hand there is value in rotating the leadership among the most committed members, or in dividing the parts among the group. The Grove should experiment widely in their first months, to better understand their skills and preferences.

As the Grove learns ritual together the strengths and weaknesses of the various members will become apparent. The work of excellent ritual will be enhanced by honest evaluation and discussion of those talents. All members should be aware of such variables as voice volume, clarity, ability to fill scripted speech with feeling, and timing. Members should be frank with one another, give and accept criticism graciously, and work earnestly to correct their own shortcomings. In some groups it will become plain that some members can best serve as ritual leaders, while in others levels of skill will be more equal.

This final phase of the second triad of the Dedicant's work flows naturally into the beginning of the third and final triad.

A Few Reminders

Before moving on to the final steps of the work, it is well to review the ongoing work of the training circle.

From the first triad, the work of study will be ongoing through out the Grove's life. From its founding onward, every member of the Grove should be encouraged to read and discuss the best, most recent and most relevant scholarship on the Grove's cultural focus. As the training circle moves on to later works it may be pleasant to move discussion of current reading to more relaxed meetings–coffee nights, etc.

Of course insights into Pagan virtues and their meaning and application in everyday life are always a proper topic for similar discussion.

In the second triad it is important for the members to pursue their individual works of meditation and shrine devotion. The occasional meetings of the training circle should not be allowed to substitute for more regular and personal work. Again, these efforts and their results make excellent topics for group discussion.

Full Ritual Worship and Basic Theurgy

If the circle has been working with simple group devotional rites, the next stage is to move on to the full Order of Ritual. If solid work has been done to develop the group's ritual skills it should be a fairly simple transition.

The Simple Rite of Offering is the easiest script with which to begin. If the circle has already worked it as part of their training, the Small Group Liturgy may be useful.

If the group feels comfortable in their writing skills they may certainly write their own basic ritual language, following the outline of the Order of Ritual. Scripts are provided to give students a model for ritual speech. They need not be followed slavishly, and can be rewritten or discarded. The outline of the Order of Ritual is all that is actually mandated.

That opens the topic of scripted versus extempore rites. There are advantages and disadvantages to both. Scripted ritual offers the chance to carefully develop ritual language, refining it through several drafts. In that way the Grove can be satisfied that the content of the rite will be focused and uplifting; however, scripts can pose several difficulties. If the group does not have strong skills in the effective presentation of written materials, the reading of a script may be dry and stilted. The need to shuffle papers, keep one's place in a script and read by candlelight creates logistical problems. These can be reduced by arranging the scripts in small booklets, or by placing individual parts on index cards to be handed to participants. Handwritten, lightly-typed or corner-stapled scripts should be avoided.

If at all possible, scripts should be memorized before the rite. This provides all the benefits of scripting without the difficulties of reading and handling. However, memorization doesn't come easily to everyone. Some members may find that the stress of performing memorized lines is more distracting than dealing with a physical script. Even when a part is being read, the member should spend time becoming very familiar with the part, and planning how to read it well.

Many groups find compromise in using a standard script for the parts of the rite that remain the same in all cases, reading from paper until memorization comes through repetition and familiarity. When that way is taken, paper scripts should be abandoned as soon as possible.

Some groups will feel more comfortable with unscripted, extempore rites. Quality performance of this sort requires a thorough familiarity with the order, symbolism and meaning of the rite, and the ability to create expressive, poetic language at will. Stumbling, clumsy speech, bad timing and errors in the Order of Ritual are the dangers in extempore rites.

Perhaps the best compromise is to begin with simple, scripted rites, performed either in unison or with parts rotated among members. That will allow all members to become familiar with a body of ritual speech. They can then draw on that base in creating extempore speech. When the new Grove can work a simple liturgy without script and with eloquence and grace, they will have finished an important step in their training.

The Inner Work of the Rites

As the new Grove learns the basics of performing our Order of Ritual, they should also be focusing on the inner, psychological and spiritual portions of the rite.

In ancient times, people grew to adulthood immersed in the religious symbols and ideas of their Pagan culture. When they attended a rite their own imaginations would supply mental content appropriate to the work at hand. Modern students bring no such store of lore with them, and so we recommend the use of guided or planned imagery to fill in that blank.

In the middle stages of training the circle will wish to work with the 'Meditative Rite of Offering', or similar exercises. Such scripts can, again, be read onto tape, or lead by various members of the circle.

Different groups will evolve different patterns of understanding for the inner and spiritual realities of our rites. We won't spend time here on detailed instruction. Instead, here are the broad categories of myth and vision that will apply to nearly every rite.

1. **The Order Of The Worlds:** In the opening sections of the Order, the Sacred Cosmos is called into being in the Grove. Members should have a store of images for the Underworld, Midrealm & Heavens, the Land, Sea & Sky, etc. This leads directly to:

2. **The Sacred Center/Gate/Boundary**: One of the central intentions of constructing the Sacred Cosmos is to create the Sacred Center, the Boundary Between All Worlds. Members should have images for this process, and a store of experiences to deepen those images.

3 **The Presence Of The Kindreds**: The members should develop a store of images of the presence of the Gods and Goddesses, the Honored Dead and the Spirits of the Land.

4 **The Presence Of The Patron Powers**: These images must be developed specifically for each rite. The members should have clear images for the Deities or Spirits that receive special offerings in any rite.

5 **Value Offered, Value Returned**: In the works of offering and sacrifice, and in the work of receiving blessing, some kind of 'energy', or means of exchange, should be envisioned. Members may envision, this as some form of energy–light, shadow, etc. –or as some more physical symbol–mead flowing, flame shining, etc.

If the members of a study circle enjoy trance-work, they may choose to incorporate guided visions into the course of ritual. This should certainly be done several times during the basic phases of training. Study circle time can also be used to practice guided visualizations focused specifically on one of these sets of images. Trances to experience the Kindreds, to grasp the mandala of the Sacred Cosmos, etc., can be valuable content for meetings, and provide fodder for later ritual experience. In addition, the work of reading and study can provide a valuable store of images directly from the tales. In reading the actual myths and tales of the ancients we can find images on which to base our modern works of vision.

As with physical forms of ritual, the group might experiment with various forms in its early work. After a time, a Grove finds traditions of symbolism and trance that work well for them.

The First Public Rites

When the study circle has worked at least a few rites in the full Order of Ritual, and worked with the inner symbols of the work, they should consider opening their Holy Day rites to the local Pagan public. The work of serving the Powers along with a community is central to ADF's vision. Our Groves are not meant to be closed circles of friends, not meant to turn faces inward in a circle. We seek to serve other Pagans, and serve the Gods and Spirits, by creating powerful opportunities for worship and blessing. Many Groves find that when they offer our work to a community, people respond happily. A well-received Grove can expect attendances of 30 - 50 even by the end of their first year.

In the first seasons it will be the members of the Grove's initial study circle who will be best qualified to lead rites. The circle should again asses their skills, and assign roles according to ability.

The first public rite should probably be one of the Holy Days, according to the calendar of the preferred culture. There are scripts available for many versions of the High Days, that have been used successfully by other Groves. They are available as resources, whether worked as written, or mined for ideas. There may be advantages to using a proven script for the first public outing.

The topic of the first public rites really deserves an article of its own. Here is a list of considerations in organizing a public rite.

Ritual Personnel

There are several ways to divide the leadership roles in our rites. Some groups name a Sacrificer, a Seer and a Bard.

* Sacrificer–does invocations, makes or supervises offerings.

* Seer–performs/manages trances and divinations

* Bard–performs/manages music, poetry & story

The group may also choose a Chief of the Rite, or a team of co-Chiefs. These handle the 'standing in the middle' part of the rite, while other parts are done by other members. Sections of the Cosmos building and Kindred Offerings can be done even by fairly new members simply and well.

Rehearsal

New Groves should certainly hold rehearsal for their early rites. There may be some resistance to the idea, and we certainly don't mean that members should 'pretend' to do sacred work. Working as leaders, and in front of guests, offers special challenges. The Grove should work to make their first liturgy smooth, competent and inspiring. Even a single walk-through rehearsal, with attention to actions, intentions and outline, will help to insure that outcome.

Location

If possible, the Grove's work should be done in a public place. Most cities have spaces available, whether in city parks, local friendly churches, community buildings or book shop meeting rooms. Such a facility allows the Grove to advertise freely, and welcome interested strangers without the issues that arise when meeting in homes. Of course many Groves must meet in homes, especially at first. It then becomes a matter of virtue how the homeowner and the Grove balance openness and hospitality with privacy and control issues. In any case, a member who hosts Grove meetings should never be allowed to gain special influence as a result.

Advertising

This will be regulated by the social climate of the Grove's region. Some areas have active local Pagan communities. In that case the Grove can do extensive outreach perhaps using flyers in local Pagan-friendly merchants. Others will need more discreet methods.

Equipment List

The Grove must insure that every item needed for the rite is available, clean and in good condition, and that it gets transported to the ritual site. If the Grove hasn't obtained larger Hallows, now is the time! Drinking vessels, platters, offerings, etc.–the leaders should read through the script or outline and be certain that everything is available as needed.

Hospitality

The Grove should arrange some simple welcome, whether coffee and biscuits or a full feast. This should not be left to the owner of the house in which the rite is held, but should be paid for by the Grove. Most Groves practice potluck feasting, though the members should plan to bear the early costs. (Note: if the Grove has collected even $5 monthly from its core group, some budget will be available!)

The Oath Of Dedication

The Dedicant's Oath was written for solitary students, aimed at those with little access to other training. The ceremonies presented were written for solo work, and will need some adaptation.

Some Groves might choose to make their group Oath Rite their first 'fully produced' Druid rite, before taking up public worship. Parts can be divided among the members, with one performing the Vertical Axis, one the Gate Opening, three the Kindreds, or whatever the numbers of the Grove will allow. The sections of the script can easily be adapted for group work.

The Oath-Offerings should probably be made individually. Perhaps each member should privately choose their offering and bring it to the rite. Each chooses something meaningful and symbolic of their path and their vision of the Pagan way.

In the same way, the group must choose whether to write a single Dedicant's Oath for the whole Grove, or allow each member to write and speak their own. Making a single Oath can help the Grove build a strong group mind, as long as each member is truly in accord with the contents of the Oath. For each member to sit in honor of the others as each gives a personal Oath can also build mutual respect and affection. It must be said that personal Oaths may greatly increase the length of the rite. The company should be prepared to sit attentively through about five minutes per member.

The Oath leads directly to the Prayer of Sacrifice. Perhaps the whole group should pronounce the final sentences of the Prayer together, whether they've made group or individual oaths and offerings. Again, the Grove may choose to make a single, corporate offering, perhaps in addition to individual sacrifices.

The Omen should perhaps be taken for each student. Perhaps each should simply draw three runes, or ogham staves, and note them. The group might then spend a few minutes in silent meditation on the Gate, the Powers and the Omen. An additional Omen might be taken for the Grove itself.

The hallowing of the Blessing can probably be divided among the group, with all joining in the final cry.

The hallowing of the tokens of Dedication might be done in unison, passing the tokens through the Fire and Water, and giving the consecration together. After the tokens are put on, a good length of silent meditation should be allowed.

This group Dedication rite might be made the occasion for celebration, followed by a Grove feast. The event should be journalized immediately, by each.

The Grove Rite of Dedication can take place either before or after the choice of Grove Patrons, culture and pantheon.

Grove Religion

The Dedicant's work requires that individuals seek alliance with deities and spirits from their primary culture to whom they will pay special devotion. We refer to these as the Hearth Gods. These patrons become the center of the personal or household religion of the individual.

In an ideal example, a Grove is formed around a single cultural complex, and the Gods and Spirits that come with it. This imaginary ideal Grove would then recruit members who are drawn to that pantheon, and do all or most of their work in that context.

However, this is often not the case. Groves attract members with widely different interests, even (or especially) in their start-up phases. Members find their way to many pantheons and cultures, and desire to have these Deities honored. A Grove is often under pressure to work rites in several cultures. The group will need to make a conscious decision whether or not to focus only on a single path.

If the organizing members of the Grove are willing to make a strict decision on a single culture, then exercises to understand the Grove Religion will be simple to devise. The Grove could swear, as a body, to honor their cultural pantheon primarily. (Groups might be advised not to swear to keep any path to the exclusion of all others. Life can lead in many unexpected directions.) If, instead, the Grove finds itself serving several pantheons it might be best to refrain from swearing to any single one.

Shining Lakes Grove has been developing a model for discovering a Grove pantheon that reflects both the traditional patterns of a Celtic tribe and the real features of the local landscape. That Grove has worked systematically to discover their local River Mother, Tribal Father etc., are, and are establishing their work based on these results. In this way they are growing a distinctive local religion that is in accord with what we know of tradition.

Remember that the building of a Grove is an organic process. We hope that these ideas can be seed, water and light for those who take up this challenging and rewarding path.

Appendix E:
Rune and Ogham Charts

Below you will find charts of Runes and Ogham for use in seeking omens, with each symbol and its basic meaning. For more in-depth and detailed meanings, consult the book list in Appendix A. Always remember that the symbols are sensitive to context, and that messages from The Mighty Ones aren't always clear upon first reading, but sometimes require reflection and time to become clear.

Runes

Freya's Aet

Fehu — Cattle, Wealth	Uruz — Bull, Strength	Thurisaz — Giant, Thor's Hammer	Ansuz — A god, Odin
Raido/Raidho — Journey	Ken/Kenaz — Torch, Flame	Gebo — Gift, Sacrifice	Wunjo — Joy, Ecstasy

Hagail's Aet

Hagalaz — Hail, Protection	Nauthiz/Naudhiz — Need fire	Isa — Ice, Solidification	Jera — Year, Harvet
Eihwaz — Yew Tree, Ancestors	Perthro — Dicecup, Merriment	Algiz/Elhaz — Axe, Protection	Sowelo/Sowilo — Sun, Victory

Tyr's Aet

Tyr/Tiwaz — Tyr, Honor	Berkana/Berkano — Birch, Woman	Ehwaz — Horse, Industry	Mannaz — Humankind
Laguz — Lake, Water	Ing/Ingwaz — Freyr, Fertility	Othila/Othala — Inheritance	Dagaz — Day

Appendices

Ogham

Beith Birch Beginnings	**Luis** Rowan Protection	**Fern** Alder Endurance	**Saill** Willow Intuition	**Nion** Ash Wisdom
hUath Hawthorn Consequence	**Dair** Oak Strength	**Tinne** Holly Action	**Coll** Hazel Creativity	**Ceirt** Apple Beauty, Love
Muin Vine Introspection	**Gort** Ivy Change	**nGeadal** Reed Harmony, Health	**Straif** Blackthorn Control	**Ruis** Elder Transition
Ailm White Fir Energy	**Onn** Gorse Transmutation	**Ur** Heather Dreams, Feelings	**Eadhadh** Poplar Victory	**Iodhadh** Yew Illusion
Eabhadh Aspen Endurance	**Or** Spindle Creativity	**Uilleann** Honeysuckle Attraction	**Ifin** Gooseberry Clear Thought	**Eamhancholl** Beech Purification